IT'S
TIME
FOR
BROTHERHOOD

by Elizabeth Hough Sechrist and Janette Woolsey

IT'S TIME TO GIVE A PLAY
NEW PLAYS FOR RED LETTER DAYS
IT'S TIME FOR THANKSGIVING
IT'S TIME FOR CHRISTMAS
IT'S TIME FOR EASTER

by Elizabeth Hough Sechrist

POEMS FOR RED LETTER DAYS
ONE THOUSAND POEMS FOR CHILDREN
THIRTEEN GHOSTLY YARNS
HEIGH-HO FOR HALLOWEEN
CHRISTMAS EVERYWHERE
RED LETTER DAYS

IT'S
TIME
FOR
BROTHERHOOD

*By Elizabeth (Hough) Sechrist
and Janette Woolsey*

Illustrations by Clifford Schule

MACRAE SMITH COMPANY: PHILADELPHIA

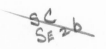

Library of Congress Catalog Card Number 62-19985
Manufactured in the United States of America
6211
Second Printing

ACKNOWLEDGMENTS

The authors wish to express their thanks to the publishers who granted permission for the quotations used in this book and to the organizations and individuals whose cooperation was greatly appreciated, as follows:

American Friends Service Committee, Inc. and Mary Esther McWhirter, Director, for material on The American Friends Service Committee; The American National Red Cross and Roy E. Johnson, Director, for material on The American National Red Cross; CARE, Inc. and Miss Alice Kapeller for material on CARE and MEDICO; The Dr. Tom Dooley Foundation, Inc. and Verne E. Chaney, M.D., Executive Field Director, for information on The Dr. Tom Dooley Foundation; Rabbi Moses N. Friedman of York, Pennsylvania, for information on the People to People program and on "Twinning"; Harper and Brothers for permission to quote from *On My Own* by Eleanor Roosevelt, published by Harper and Brothers, 1958; The People to People Health Foundation, Inc. and Miss Carol Le Varn, Director of Public Relations, for material on Project Hope; The Macmillan Company for permission to quote from *Twenty Years at Hull-House* by Jane Addams, published by The Macmillan Company, 1935, and *On the Edge of the Primeval Forest,* by Albert Schweitzer, translated by C. T. Campion and published by The Macmillan Company, 1931; The National Conference of Christians and Jews, Inc. and Mrs. Elizabeth D. Norris, Librarian, for material on The National Conference of Christians and Jews; Fleming H. Revell Company for permission to quote from *General Evangeline Booth* by P. Whitwell Wilson, published by Fleming H. Revell Company, 1935; United Nations Library and Harry N. M. Winton, Acting Chief, Documents Reference Section, for information on the Nansen Passports; *United Nations Review* and J. Robert Herbin, Editor-in-Chief, for permission to quote from an article by Maurice Pate, Director of Children's Fund, in the *United Nations Review.*

To
Davia Ann and Kate Emerson Wood
and
Hallett B. and Gertrude Hough Hammatt

Contents

CONTENTS

IT'S
TIME
FOR
BROTHERHOOD

A mystic bond of brotherhood makes all men one.
—THOMAS CARLYLE

"WHO IS MY NEIGHBOR?"
—LUKE 10:29

In this book we want to explore the subject of the brotherhood of man, something of its history up to this time, and how it is being recognized in our world.

Many contributions to the cause of brotherhood have been made by great men and women who have been unwavering in their belief that every individual is a member of one human family, regardless of his race, color or creed. Some of these lived and left their mark upon the world long ago; some of them are living today. We shall see that many of them struggled alone under great difficulties in carrying out their beliefs. Others established or worked for organizations that have served mankind.

Brotherhood might be defined as a state of fellowship between a man and his neighbor. In ancient times, a man's neighbors were the people of his tribe or village. But in our world today, with communications drawing men ever closer, our neighbors are all men everywhere, however far away they may live.

The idea of man's responsibility to his neighbor is not a new one. As a matter of fact, we find that it is a part of many of the great religions of the world. The Christian religion is based on the teachings of Jesus Christ. His commandment, "Thou shalt love thy neighbor as thyself," expresses the spirit of all human brotherhood. When Jesus preached in Jerusalem He was asked by a lawyer, "Who is my neighbor?" And Jesus, in a parable, illustrated what He meant by one's neighbor. This is the story of the good Samaritan and is recorded in St. Luke:

> And Jesus answering said, "A certain man went down from Jerusalem to Jericho, and fell among thieves, which stripped him

of his raiment, and wounded him, and departed, leaving him half dead. And by chance there came down a certain priest that way: and when he saw him, he passed by on the other side. And likewise a Levite, when he was at the place, came and looked on him, and passed by on the other side. But a certain Samaritan, as he journeyed, came where he was: and when he saw him, he had compassion on him. And went to him, and bound up his wounds, pouring in oil and wine, and set him on his own beast, and brought him to an inn, and took care of him. And on the morrow when he departed, he took out two pence, and gave them to the host, and said unto him, 'Take care of him; and whatsoever thou spendest more, when I come again, I will repay thee.'

"Which now of these three, thinkest thou, was neighbor unto him that fell among the thieves?"

And he said, "He that showed mercy on him."

Then said Jesus unto him, "Go, and do thou likewise."

The words spoken by Moses, the leader and teacher of the Jews, thousands of years ago, and recorded in the Bible, are still used today in the first prayer learned by a Jewish child: "Hear, O Israel, The Lord our God, the Lord is one." When Moses was commanded by God to write the Ten Commandments, these included laws concerning man and his neighbor. Now the Jewish people to whom the laws of Moses are sacred live in almost every country in the world. Many wise teachings of men of the Jewish faith are recorded in another book, *Sayings of the Fathers.* One of these tells of a man named Hillel who was challenged by a Roman to teach him the entire Jewish religion while standing on one foot. Hillel's answer is a well-known precept: "Do not do unto others what thou wouldst not do unto thyself. This is the whole law; all else is commentary (related to it)."

One of the most ancient moral instructors was Confucius, a great teacher and scholar who lived and taught in China in the sixth century before Christ. Above all, Confucius taught *jen,* right relationships between men. Among the collections of his sayings and rules of good conduct is the rule of loving-kindness: "Do not unto others what you do not want done unto you."

Another of the great wise men of China was Lao-Tzu, who lived at the same time as Confucius. He taught humility and obedience to the balancing laws of nature, which he called *Tao,* the way. Among his suggestions for following *Tao* was this one: "Regard your neighbor's gain as your own gain and likewise his loss as your own loss." Also, "Avoid putting yourself before others and you can become a leader among men." These two Chinese philosophers believed that if man is just he will not want to put himself above his neighbor.

It was about this time, also, that a great teacher arose in India. His name was Siddhartha Gautama, but he became known as Buddha, the Enlightened One. He acquired this name because, after many years of searching, he found what he knew to be the true meaning of life. After his death many of his precepts were written down by his followers. One of these was, "Cleanse your heart of malice and cherish no hatred, not even against your enemies; but embrace all living beings with kindness." The order of monks founded by Buddha spent nine months of each year teaching his precepts to the people. They taught that all men are brothers, whether born in high places or low, whether rich or poor.

Even older than Buddhism is Hinduism, the religion of most Indians today. It is founded on a belief in a universal divine spirit, which the Hindus call Brahman. One of their rules of conduct is, "Do naught unto others which would cause you pain if done unto you."

One-seventh of the entire world's population is composed of people who practice the religion of Islam. They call themselves Moslems, include people of many races, colors and nationalities, and consider themselves brothers under one faith. Their teacher, Mohammed, was born in Mecca in the year 571 A.D. The people among whom Mohammed lived worshiped many gods, and he sensed that this was wrong. He spent a great deal of time meditating and, when he was forty years old, he had visions in which he heard a voice telling him that he was a prophet and that he must preach. Mohammed eventually became ruler, law-giver and commander of his people. Before he died he had seen the Arabs give up idolatry and become worshipers of Allah, the one God. One of the precepts taught by Mohammed was this: "No one is a true believer until he desires for his brother that which he desires for himself."

Many demonstrations of brotherhood and neighborliness will be found in the pages of this book, and most of them took place in our own times. One of the most inspiring is the story of the Four Chaplains. The act of sacrifice of these four men of different faiths exemplifies the true spirit of brotherhood.

The four chaplains

The four men who were chaplains boarded the U.S. Troopship *Dorchester* that night in January, 1943, unaware that they were to become heroes. They knew, as the soldiers who were boarding her did not, that the *Dorchester* was bound for the icy shores of a desolate destination, Greenland. Not one of them, in offering his services to his country, had visualized himself in such an isolated spot. When they met together in the cabin they were to share below decks, they agreed that the soldiers who had been given this assignment would perhaps need more moral support than those who were being sent into the thick of battle. Later, when they mingled with the soldiers and spoke cheering words to them, it wasn't difficult to read their thoughts, and sense the fear and apprehension among them. An unknown destination, and on such a ship! She was only a five-thousand-ton craft—an old, creaky, converted freighter that had seen better days. Wherever she was bound, there was nothing about her to give these young green-horns the feeling that she'd carry them there safely.

At that time during World War II, the North Atlantic was a place of peril. Ships were being sunk by Nazi U-boats almost as fast as they ventured on the seas. Even those in large convoys with impressive escorts were being attacked. And here was the little *Dorchester* in a small convoy, her only escorts three Coast Guard cutters. No wonder anxiety and dread filled the hearts of her passengers. Each one of the chaplains was fully aware of his responsibilities and of the hazards facing them all.

The four chaplains were George Lansing Fox, Methodist; Alexander D. Goode, Jewish; John P. Washington, Catholic; Clark V. Poling, Reformed Church of America. Each man had followed his own particular path leading him to the *Dorchester*. With varying in-

15

fluences and motives, each one of them had prepared himself in his early life for the circumstance that placed him, as a man of God, upon this ship.

George Fox, the Methodist Chaplain, was the eldest of the four. He had served in the first World War. Although he had not completed high school when he enlisted and served in the Army that first time, he was determined, when he came out, to finish his education and become a minister of God. It had been a long, hard pull to get the education he needed to achieve his purpose. There were many years of struggling, working by day and going to school by night. It was not until 1934 that he finally ended his training and was ordained. But to George this was only a beginning, for he visualized a long life of preaching and serving his people. He had a strong sense of duty, and when war came again while he was pastor of a church in Gilman, Connecticut, he enlisted. He entered the service on the same day as his son. He was sent to the Chaplains' School at Harvard University. His first assignment was Greenland.

Alexander Goode, the Jewish Chaplain, had always been a fine scholar. When he was in High School he discovered that he had a talent for oratory. Later, through the influence of the rabbi of his Washington (D.C.) Hebrew Congregation, he decided to become a rabbi. One thing that made this life appeal to him was the fact that he had always been drawn to people and their problems. Through the years of the Depression he worked hard for his education, waiting on tables, tutoring and even finding time for volunteer work. In 1937 after his education was completed, he went to York, Pennsylvania, to become the rabbi of Temple Beth Israel. He was more than pleased with this charge because York was close enough to Johns Hopkins University in Baltimore for him to work there for his doctorate. When he preached his trial sermon in York it was significant that he used as his theme "Love and Faith," the two things most necessary in the life of man. He pointed out that it was man's love of God which led him to love of his fellow men; and that it was his faith in God that gave man the desire to serve humanity. He was accepted by the congregation. Later on, he received his doctorate as he had planned. The beginning of World War II found him a very busy man taking a vital part in the community life of York. When he enlisted in the Army he was sent to the Chaplains' School at Harvard for a month's training. In January of 1943 he embarked from Massachusetts on the U.S. AT *Dorchester.*

John Washington, as a lad, resented having to wear eyeglasses; but, loving sports, he learned to become a good catcher in baseball because of the mask which protected his eyes. In other ways, through his young life, John overcame unavoidable difficulties by conscious effort, trying to make a success of everything he attempted. While he was an altar boy in his home church he began to feel the meaning behind the prayers he recited. By the time he was in seventh grade he had made up his mind to become a priest. During the years of study and retreat, he became ever more aware of the opportunities for service the priesthood would offer him. He served his first Mass with a sense of deep consecration. When Pearl Harbor was bombed he was serving at St. Stephen's Church in Arlington, New Jersey. He immediately decided to enlist. And when he was turned down by the Navy because of his weak eyes, he tried the Army. To his great satisfaction he was accepted. Soon after receiving his training as a chaplain, he received his orders for overseas duty. His assignment was Greenland.

Clark V. Poling was the son of a brilliant churchman, Dr. Daniel A. Poling, founder of the Christian Endeavor in America and editor of the *Christian Herald Magazine.* The family was a close-knit one where love and consideration for others were a family heritage. While Clark was little, tragedy struck the family when his mother died. During a year spent with his grandparents he discovered the joys of reading. Later, in his college days, he wrote a great deal, mostly poetry. His summers were spent happily at the family summer home in New Hampshire and it was during this time he learned to know and love his second mother. After college he entered and later was graduated from Yale Divinity School. He was called to the First Reformed Church in Schenectady, New York. There with his wife and child he spent several happy years, working hard for his church but aware meanwhile of the unrest in the nations of the world. In his church bulletin he expressed his belief that what the world needed was "the triumphant spirit of human courage and sacrifice." When the war broke out, Clark Poling was determined at first to serve as an ordinary soldier. But his father convinced him that he could do the most good as a chaplain. He entered training and finally found himself at Camp Myles Standish in Massachusetts. From there his unit received orders: they were to be shipped to Greenland.

Conditions on the *Dorchester* for most of the men were almost unbearable. The vast majority of them were not only seasick but homesick as well. The quarters were so crowded that the air was stifling, but the icy chill of the winds on deck kept them below most of the time. Even those who tried to be cheerful were fear-ridden, and the main topic of conversation was how far they would get before the ancient craft would be torpedoed. They had been ordered to keep their life jackets with them day and night. In their minds they saw themselves a ready target for the Nazi submarines they felt were surrounding them. In spite of all the four chaplains could do to try to give courage to the men, they all felt they were living in a nightmare.

Finally on the second of February, the men's worst fears were confirmed. Out of the darkness one of the escorts flashed a signal to the *Dorchester* that a submarine was following her. The next day a Canadian patrol plane flew over. Quickly, the *Dorchester* blinked out a message for assistance. But as quickly the reply was returned: *Planes on duty elsewhere.* That night after "chow," with forced cheer born of desperation, the men decided to have a party. They brought an old, dilapidated piano into the mess hall and soon were lustily singing popular songs interspersed with hymns. It was an odd night, with fear riding high on the *Dorchester* in spite of the bravado the men tried to show. But somehow the night passed. The following day the troopship pulled into the pier at St. John's, Newfoundland. Here, for a time, the men felt secure. That evening the *Dorchester* was on her way again through the icy waters bound for Greenland.

In the night the captain reduced the speed of the ship because she was running through ice. Somehow the thought of ice was a relief to the soldiers because they thought there was less chance of submarines. But the weather grew stormy, causing the *Dorchester* to be buffeted about on her tortuous crawl onward. Then, directly after the ship's bell sounded one o'clock, a torpedo struck. It tore into the engine room and a hundred men died. The others struggled through the blackness trying to get to the upper decks, terror in their hearts. A boiler blew up, adding to the horror and confusion. Up on deck, some in their frenzy had plunged overboard into the icy waters. Others came on deck without their life jackets and, going back for them, perished in the steam-filled holds below. Soldiers who were only boys were weeping, and everywhere the crowds were pushing, crying out, and screaming for help. In all the chaos, the lifeboats—those that were not listing too far inboard to be freed—were somehow lowered and filled to overflowing with men.

But out of the mad rush of men, some emerged who were filled with courage. The captain of the ship issued commands in a last vital effort to save every man possible. Medical men worked frantically to help the injured who were being brought up from below. The four chaplains were everywhere, helping men into the boats, trying to prevent others from jumping into the sea, giving words of courage to those who were too paralyzed with fear to think for themselves.

When it was apparent to all that the *Dorchester* was steadily being sucked down and that all who stayed would go down with her, unreasoning terror seized the men. Now the four chaplains stood together and urged the men to leave the ship before it was too late. They handed out life jackets as long as there were any left, and when there were no more they removed their own jackets and placed them on others. "Take it; I won't need it," were the words as the chaplains gave up their chance to live.

Those who survived the sinking of the *Dorchester* remember the last glimpse they had of the four chaplains, arms linked together, standing on the deck of the old troopship as she rapidly sank down to her watery grave. Protestants, Catholic and Jew, they had followed their God and loved their brothers in full measure, even to the last supreme sacrifice. "Greater love hath no man than this."

part **II**
SERVING THEIR NEIGHBORS

SERVING THEIR NEIGHBORS

Give me your tired, your poor,
Your huddled masses yearning to breathe free,
The wretched refuse of your teeming shore,
Send these, the homeless, tempest-tossed, to me:
I lift my lamp beside the golden door.

—EMMA LAZARUS'S VERSE ON THE
STATUE OF LIBERTY, NEW YORK

In our world today we are facing new problems all the time. But all our problems are not new ones. Some of them have existed since the late eighteen hundreds when the immigration laws were less strict. At that time thousands upon thousands of people from other countries teemed through the open door of America. Often they concentrated in the big cities where they hoped to make a living. Many of these hardworking people did succeed and some made fortunes, but the first years were very hard for them. Often they were so destitute that only by their courage and determination were they able to live at all. They and their children needed help. Most of all they needed a friend.

The biographies that follow are of some who lent a helping hand when it was sorely needed. They awakened other Americans to the need for social work.

Jacob August Riis: brother to all men

Theodore Roosevelt, a great American President, once referred to Jacob Riis as a "brother to all men." And indeed he deserved the tribute—this man who had experienced personally many of the hardships that befall unfortunate people. By his untiring efforts he wiped out some of the worst living conditions existing in New York's lower East Side slums.

Jacob Riis did not start life as an American citizen. He was born May 3, 1849, in Ribe, Denmark. Ribe was really an old world city. It was not one to accept new ideas and kept to the customs of the past. Whale-oil lanterns were in use—and lamps burning the dangerous coal-oil which some cities were importing from America. People still carried tinderboxes instead of matches to light fires. Stagecoaches rumbled over cobbled streets and watchmen called out the hour of night. Indeed, people would have been most uncomfortable if they had not been awakened every hour to be told all was well.

Jacob's father was a respected schoolmaster in Ribe and was greatly disappointed when Jacob didn't follow in his footsteps. In writing of his own life in later years, Jacob said he hated school from the very first day. And no doubt the experience he had that first day would make anyone hate it. On arriving at school he was led into the school yard by his teacher and thrust into an empty hogshead (a large cask). That was where he would be put, she told the frightened child sternly, if he was ever bad!

When Jacob was fourteen years old he persuaded his father to let him leave school. Although his father was very reluctant to do so, he apprenticed him to a carpenter in Ribe, as Jacob insisted that was the work he wanted to do. After serving his apprenticeship there, he went to Copenhagen for four years to complete his training.

Now Jacob had other reasons besides his dislike of school to start earning his living. In the first place he was the third child in a family that eventually numbered fifteen, and he felt he wanted to take care of himself. And there was something else too. Ever since he was a little boy he had been determined that someday he was going to marry the lovely, curly-haired blonde, Elizabeth Gjortz. But Elizabeth's father, a wealthy factory owner, had more ambitious plans for his daughter and discouraged Jacob's attentions. Elizabeth, too, was persuaded that it was foolish to accept Jacob's proposal, although she wept as she refused him.

Jacob thereupon resolved that the thing to do was to get as far away from Ribe as possible. He decided to seek his fortune in America. The year he was twenty-one he sailed for the New World with only enough money for steerage passage. Just before he left, his friends gave him a purse with forty dollars which constituted his total wealth. But with him he carried something most precious. Elizabeth's mother, more sympathetic than her father, had given him as a parting gift a locket which enclosed a lock of Elizabeth's hair.

The young immigrant from Denmark, full of ambition and enthusiasm, found disappointment waiting for him on the shores of the New World. New York City, like most large cities, was a place of contrasts. There was the New York of Fifth Avenue with its magnificent homes, and there was the lower East Side with its appalling slums.

When Jacob was in Copenhagen he might have noticed that there was overcrowding in that city too. But, probably because he did not have to share in those conditions, he was not conscious of them. At least he makes no mention of them in the account of his life in that city.

But New York was different. Here he was a penniless stranger and forced to come into contact with all that was sordid and unhappy. When he was unable to find work in New York he tried to find employment many other places. He signed up with an iron works in western Pennsylvania and was sent out there. The job didn't last very long and for one day he was a coal miner. But he knew that this type of work was not for him and so by doing odd jobs he made his way back to New York. It was during the period after his return that he came to know the worst of New York's evil slums.

New York's lower East Side had once been the residential section of well-to-do families. But gradually they had moved uptown and what had once been beautiful homes were now wretched tenement houses. Large rooms had been divided and the inside ones had neither light nor ventilation. Sometimes floors were added one on top of the other with no consideration as to whether the foundation below could stand the extra height.

Other tenements were built behind those facing the street and they were even worse. Their rooms could hardly be dignified by calling them that. They were more like cubbyholes. One which Riis described as housing a family of three was so small that a person could not take more than three steps in any direction!

There was no incentive for people to keep such places clean and most of the people living in them had no desire to, anyway. In fact, these filthy conditions were not only accepted by the landlords but were even encouraged. The worse things got, the more excuse the landlords had not to repair or clean up the dwellings.

Thousands of people lived in cellars. The streets were crowded with tramps and beggars. Children were not made to go to school and there was a great deal of juvenile crime. And of course the greatest evil that came out of all of this unclean living was the disease that spread rapidly. Terrible epidemics were common.

Even the names of the streets help paint the picture of what it must have been like: Mulberry Bend, Bottle Alley, Bandit's Roost, Bone Alley, Thieves' Alley, Kerosene Row, Hell's Kitchen and Poverty Gap.

Pushcarts which sold everything from food to clothing jammed the streets. Most of the work done by these poor people was in the overcrowded tenement rooms. Sometimes as many as twelve persons worked at sewing in a single small room that was also the living quarters of an entire family. Even children were put to work as soon as they were old enough to draw a thread.

In hot weather it became so unbearable that people slept on roofs, fire escapes, trucks and even window sills.

Something this young Danish lad found that horrified him even more was the ill-famed police lodging house. Police officers at that time, operating under a corrupt city government, were not noted for humane treatment to those who were unfortunate. Each night they opened a room and let tramps sleep there on wooden planks. The only cleaning the place ever got was what they called "bed-making" which consisted in once in a while turning the planks over. Needless to say, these rooms were infested with all sorts of vermin.

Young Riis, completely penniless, had to seek lodging there one night. He had with him, under his coat, a homeless little mongrel who had attached himself to him. When the policeman in charge saw the dog he told Riis to leave it outside. Sometime during the night Riis discovered that he had been robbed of his precious locket containing the lock of Elizabeth's hair. He reported it to an officer, whose only reply was to kick him out the door. The little dog, which had been waiting patiently on the steps for his new master, seized the policeman by the ankle. To Riis's utter horror the policeman killed his dog right before him. Then and there he resolved that someday he would expose that sort of brutality.

Utterly disheartened, he made his way to Philadelphia and in desperation applied to the Danish Consul for help. From this time things took a turn for the better. The consul arranged for him to get transportation to a little town near Buffalo, New York, where there were a number of Danish people living. He started several business ventures but none of them was successful, and finally he decided to try New York once more. By this time he knew definitely what he wanted to do: somehow he must get a job on a newspaper.

Unsuccessful at first, he tried his hand at selling books. And appropriately enough, the first book he was given to sell was *Hard Times* by Charles Dickens!

One day he met by chance an old friend who told him of an opening in a news-gathering agency. To his great satisfaction he got the job at the enormous salary of ten dollars a month.

From that time on he never left the writing field. He was offered a job on a paper in Brooklyn, and later, when the owners decided they wanted to sell it, he persuaded them to let him buy it. That meant borrowing money, but Jacob worked hard and it was not very long before he had his debt paid.

About this time, he learned from one of his mother's letters that Elizabeth Gjortz was still single. He decided to write to her once more and ask her to be his wife. As months went by he despaired of ever hearing from her—and then one day the letter came. To his everlasting joy she had accepted. At first he wrote her that he would be over to marry her in a year. Then he told her it would be in the spring. The next letter mentioned the winter; the next, the early winter—and in the end he sold his paper and took the first boat he could. Jacob and

Elizabeth were married in the little church at Ribe with practically all the townspeople in attendance. Immediately afterward, Jacob brought his bride back to America.

Jacob Riis had always wanted a job with the *New York Tribune,* and not long after he arrived back in New York he was offered one at a salary of $25 a week. His assignment was Police Headquarters. Now he had the chance he had been waiting for. He could report on crimes and how they were being handled by the police. It was the duty of police reporters to gather news of murders, fires and robberies before they came to court. These reporters were not very popular with the police, who didn't want publicity on crimes they couldn't solve, and there was a sort of contest, with the police trying to conceal the news and the reporters trying to ferret it out.

Riis had not been on this assignment very long before he found out that there was an organization of citizens working against the police lodging houses, so he joined it. At first the other members were a little suspicious when they found that a newsman was working with them. But they soon found out that he could give their campaign what it needed most—publicity. Article after article he wrote. Some civic leaders began to sit up and take notice. And then something happened that aroused all the citizens. Typhus broke out—a dreaded disease that was often fatal. Riis went to the Board of Health and complained that the lodging houses were helping to spread the disease. When the Board wouldn't listen to him, he took pictures of the lodging houses, made them into slides and took them to the Academy of Medicine to show to the doctors. And he wrote more and more stories for his paper about the terrible living conditions in the slums.

Soon after this the aroused citizens voted the corrupt city officials out of office and a new reform government came in. Along with this new government came Theodore Roosevelt, who was appointed President of the Police Court. When Riis took Roosevelt on a tour of the lodging houses the horrified Roosevelt promised that they would be closed, and he was as good as his word. The very next day he took action. The police lodging house was a thing of the past.

About this time there was an invention which helped Riis to present his stories in a more dramatic fashion—the flash-light camera. At the risk of his life he got into some of the awful tenement houses he had been describing and took pictures of rooms that had been too dark to photograph before. More and more people began to read his illustrated articles and the public conscience was aroused.

Finally the city began to take action. Building after building was torn down. But the clean-up job wasn't easy; opposition came from all directions. First of all there were the landlords. They complained loudly over their loss of revenue and demanded payments far more than their buildings were worth. Some people thought that citizens were losing their rights because the city had condemned their properties, and they voiced objections. And then there were the tenants themselves: some had to be bodily removed from the cellars where they had hidden. But at last the buildings were torn down and in their place a park came into being. With the whole area opened to sunshine and fresh air, it seemed as though the whole character of the section was changed.

Riis's articles began to appear in magazines and then were expanded into books, *How the Other Half Lives* and *The Battle with the Slums*. Everywhere Riis was in demand as a lecturer, and he carried his plea for better housing wherever he could. It was not just housing he worked for, either. The plight of New York's children was of great concern to him. He fought for new schools, new playgrounds and better treatment of wayward children. When illness and death came to Jacob Riis in 1914, he was mourned by many for his reforms which benefited so many people.

Edward Bulwer Lytton once wrote, "The pen is mightier than the sword." Living proof of this was Jacob August Riis, "brother to all men."

Jane Addams and Hull-House

The name of Jane Addams, during and after her lifetime, was blessed by countless people, while the words Hull-House spelled magic to many thousands of others who had come under its protection or taken part in its busy life. Jane Addams was the founder of Hull-House, the first social settlement in America, which began a whole new era in social work and made Jane Addams famous not only in Chicago and the United States but abroad as well.

In her book *Twenty Years at Hull-House,* Jane Addams tells of the first time she became conscious that poverty existed. She was happily riding one day with her father in the family horse-drawn buggy to the mill at Freeport where her father was to transact business. They had passed the part of the city familiar to Jane with its many exciting shops and schools and churches. They had gone through the residential section where there were attractive homes with porches and wide lawns and trees. But now they were coming to the shabby streets where the mill was located, and Jane noticed that the houses here were very small and close together, with the paint peeling off or no paint at all. There were no trees or shrubs or lawns and the people who stood about on the sidewalks were careworn and poorly dressed. "Jenny," who was less than seven years old, had never guessed that such houses existed.

"Why do they, Papa?" she asked. "Why do they live in such horrid houses?"

Her father explained that some people could not afford to live in a large house like their own, to which the little girl replied, "When I grow up I'll live in a large house like ours, but I'll have it built right in the middle of lots of horrid little houses like these. And I will let the poor people come to my home and be my neighbors."

It was a prophecy that came true.

Jane Addams was born in Cedarville, Illinois, on September 6, 1860. She was the eighth child of John H. and Sarah Addams. Four of the children had died as infants and when Jenny was two years old her mother died. At that time her eldest sister Mary was seventeen and there were two other sisters and a brother. Polly, the nurse, helped Mary to raise the children, and there were a hired girl and a hired man and a woman who washed and ironed for the family. This was the Addams household during Jenny's early childhood.

Mr. Addams was a member of the Illinois State Legislature. It was while he was away at the state capital at Springfield that he received a letter from Mary telling of little Jenny's serious illness. She had fallen ill with typhoid fever. The disease left Jane Addams with a crooked back and delicate health that was to plague her through most of the rest of her life.

Jenny adored her father. He was tall and handsome, of such fine appearance that the little girl imagined that she would bring disgrace upon him if people knew he was the father of such an unattractive daughter. She wrote in her book later:

"I prayed with all my heart that the ugly, pigeon-toed little girl, whose crooked back obliged her to walk with her head held very much upon one side, would never be pointed out to these visitors as the daughter of this fine man."

One thing she admired tremendously in her father was his "miller's thumb." In his earlier years he had been a miller by trade and had acquired a flat thumb from feeling the wheat between his thumb and forefinger. Little Jenny would sit for long periods at the mill rubbing the wheat between her thumb and finger, hoping that she, too, could have a thumb like her father's.

When Jenny was less than five years old, something happened that she was never to forget. As she went out to the front yard to play one day, she saw that the two white posts at the gate were draped in black. She ran quickly into the house to ask why. To her surprise she found her tall father with his head bent, weeping. To her questions he replied, "President Lincoln, the greatest man in the world, is dead." Jane Addams, small as she was, sensed the tragedy that the words carried. All her life she was to admire and be influenced by Abraham Lincoln's great love for humanity.

Another time her father pointed out to her a lesson in equality. She had just been given a handsome new cloak, quite the most beautiful piece of clothing she had ever owned. On the Sunday morning following this acquisition, she donned it to wear to Sunday school and presented herself in it to her father.

"It's very pretty," he said, "but I would like you to wear your old cloak to Sunday school." Trying not to show her disappointment, Jenny asked why. "We must agree it's far prettier than any the other little girls will wear today," her father said, "but for that very reason it might make the others feel badly."

This made Jenny think seriously of the fact that some little girls had pretty clothes, while others did not. She asked her father about this while they were walking to Sunday school, and he explained that there were other, more important things that people could be equal in, things like religion and education.

About this same time, when Jenny was eight, her father remarried. Her new stepmother had two sons, Harry and George. The older son attended a school in Europe, but George, who was about Jenny's age, seemed truly like a new brother. They soon became inseparable. Jenny suddenly became a tomboy, going everywhere that George went and trying to do everything that George did. They went to the mill together and played with the boys whose farmer fathers brought their wheat to be ground into flour. They fished in the mill-pond and raced through the fields and woodlands together, and Jenny's new outdoor life brought roses to her cheeks.

Jenny and George read together, too. Books were plentiful in their father's library and in the big living room. They found an old copy of the Vulgate, a book of the Scriptures written in Latin. From it they learned, word for word, the Lord's prayer in Latin, which they repeated every night. In later years when Jane was in college, she was glad she had read so much from these wonderful books of history and the classics, even though she had been partly prompted by the payment she received for doing so! Her father had paid her five cents for each life of *Plutarch's Lives* she read, and as much as a quarter each for the volumes of *The Life of Washington Irving*.

And so passed Jenny Addams's childhood.

In 1877 when Jane, as she came to be known, was seventeen, she entered Rockford Seminary as her older sisters had done. The enrollment was two hundred girls, and the tuition, including room and board, was $175 a year! Jane soon settled happily into the routine of the boarding school. She and her roommate had made their room attractive with the rugs, pillows and other things they had brought from home. Up at seven, the first girl out of bed had to light the fire in the stove. Stove ashes had to be carried out, the room made clean and the water pitcher filled each morning. Besides these chores, each girl had an hour's housework to do each day. This rule was typical of the boarding schools of the day.

Jane was a serious scholar and worked hard. At the end of her first summer vacation she took back to school with her some great, thick books on science to read, because she had decided that she would eventually become a woman doctor and minister to the poor. In her senior year at Rockford Seminary Jane was president of her class and Editor of the *Rockford Seminary Magazine*. At graduation she was valedictorian.

During the summer that followed, Jane passed through the bitter experience of her father's sudden death. Though she entered the Woman's Medical College of Philadelphia in the fall, she seemed unable to recover from the shock of her loss. After a short time she became ill and was taken as a patient to a Philadelphia hospital, suffering from her old back ailment. There followed six months of confinement to her bed in the home of her married sister. When she was up and about again, she decided to take her doctor's advice and spend the next two years in Europe trying to recover her health. And so her medical education ended, but she was destined for a different career.

There were eight in the group sailing from New York, including Jane's stepmother. They went first to Ireland and Scotland, then to England, and it was in London that Jane became painfully aware of how the really poverty-stricken people of the world lived. Her group was taken to the slums of East London to witness a scene which took place every Saturday at midnight. Because of a strict law in London, no sales were permitted on Sunday. At midnight, crowds of poor people pushed and jostled their way to the hucksters' carts to buy the leftover vegetables that were to be auctioned off. Jane had never dreamed that such people as these could be living in the world's greatest city! The most miserable of creatures, they were desperate for a chance at the cheap food that might, for another day at least, help in the constant battle to sustain themselves. As the party of onlookers watched, a head of wilted cabbage was held up for sale. Instantly, a myriad of work-worn, thin, dirty hands reached high in a pleading gesture while the ha'pennies were bid for the unsavory food. As each piece of cabbage and carrots and potatoes was sold, the greedy hands reached up desperately and grabbed the prize. Pinched, starved faces shone pitifully in the dim gaslights of the street, while the pathetic figures of other ill-clad men and women hovered close, hoping to snatch at some part of the food that might fall to the ground. The lean, groping hands reaching up stayed in Jane Addams's memory for as long as she lived.

During the two years she spent in Europe she could not shake off the thought of the millions of undernourished people of the world. For the first time she began to think of the futility of the kind of life she and others like her were living. But it was not until a later trip to Europe that she began to formulate a plan whereby she could change her life and give it purpose. Now twenty-seven, she was an attractive young woman who was mistress of a fair-sized fortune left to her by her father. While she was in Munich, Germany, she met her college friend Ellen Starr, and they decided to settle down and study Italian. While they were traveling in Italy together, Jane was laid low for several weeks with an illness and had plenty of time to think. She conceived the idea of going back to America and renting a house in the poorer section of Chicago, to give girls like herself the opportunity to work with the underprivileged. Ellen Starr not only received her plan with enthusiasm, but agreed to go along with her.

Before Jane returned to the United States she went back to London and visited Toynbee Hall, the first social settlement house in the world. There she picked up many ideas for the settlement house she was to establish in America.

In the spring of 1889 Jane and Ellen found the house they were looking for in Chicago. It was known as Hull-House because it had been built by Mr. Charles J. Hull in 1856. It had been a beautiful house in its day, and even now, among its less impressive surroundings, the red brick house looked quite handsome with its tall pillars and broad porches. It was near the corner of Halsted and Polk Streets, and its first floor was occupied as offices by a furniture factory, while there were rooms to let on the second floor. The third floor was unoccupied, probably because of its reputation for being haunted. Jane arranged to rent the large former drawing room on the first floor and all of the second floor.

This was the house that little Jenny had predicted she would have when she grew up: a "large house in the middle of lots of horrid houses." This was Hull-House, situated between a saloon and an undertaker's parlor. It was a shabby neighborhood, the home of the foreign-born of Chicago's West Side—Italians, Germans, Swiss, French, Scandinavians, Irish, and Jews from Russia and Poland. It was exactly the location Jane Addams was looking for to establish her settlement house.

The business of repairing the house and furnishing it was to extend through future years. The very next spring the settlement acquired the entire house, which ultimately expanded to thirteen buildings covering the whole city block.

With the repairs finished and the furniture moved in, Jane Addams and Ellen Starr were justly proud of Hull-House. Their own handsome furniture and treasures brought from Europe graced the rooms, and with fires burning in the open fireplaces, the house held a charm and a warmth felt by many thousands of all races and creeds coming under its spell in the years to follow.

On September 14, 1889, the two young women and a housekeeper moved into Hull-House. All three were so tired that first night that they went to bed leaving the door open; but in spite of the neighborhood's reputation, nothing was disturbed.

At first, as they had anticipated, the neighbors were suspicious of them. But it wasn't difficult to overcome the doubts about the two new, strange ladies. When some of the Italian women were invited there for tea, they came away marveling that Miss Addams and Miss Starr could converse with them in Italian! Soon after, a reading circle was formed with Ellen Starr as leader and the first book they read was *Romola* by George Eliot. Then an elderly lady who actually was their first "resident" started reading Hawthorne to the club. Perhaps the young women who attended were drawn more by the social hour held afterward than by the reading, but they came and enjoyed it. Many visitors started coming daily to Hull-House and volunteers began to offer their services to work with the classes and clubs that were being formed. Soon a kindergarten was started, and then a college extension class for ambitious young people.

It wasn't long before Jane Addams was being asked by the neighbors to visit the sick, wash newborn infants and prepare the dead for burial. There was no doubt about it: the neighborhood had accepted her.

At the end of the first year, Jane Addams, figuring expenses, found that the settlement had cost two thousand dollars. Though she and Ellen Starr had financed Hull-House at first themselves, they soon found it necessary to accept funds from interested friends. One big help was the donation rent-free of the whole house by the owner. In those first months Jane and Ellen saved money by washing the floors and cleaning the windows themselves.

After that first year, Hull-House was overrun with people of all ages. The little ones came there to kindergarten, the older children attended their clubs there in the afternoons and the old people came in the evenings, and the teen-agers were all over the building with their clubs and classes and dramatic activities. The doors of Hull-House were open to all. Some of the young women decided to save on their living expenses by joining forces and renting a large apartment together. This was the beginning of the Jane Club which later had a whole building of its own.

Hull-House was beginning to make its influence felt in Chicago. The three baths in the basement that were always open to the public led to the establishment of the first free bath houses in the city. The Chicago Public Library opened a branch in Hull-House. Persuasion by and pressure from the Men's Club at Hull-House was often the means of closing a gambling establishment or paving a street or instituting some civic improvement such as a public playground.

At the time of the opening of Hull-House, Chicago had not yet started its Charity Organization Society nor the Visiting Nurse Association. There were no unions as such. But it was at Hull-House that the women shirtmakers met and formed a union because they had been cut down to making collars and cuffs on men's shirts for twelve cents a dozen! Labor conditions in the big cities at this time were at their worst. Whole families had to be employed to make a bare living. Children were taken from school and put to work as soon as they were big enough to operate the factory machines. Sweatshops were common, with men, women and children working in crowded, unventilated, poorly-lit rooms from dawn to dark, six days a week. Mothers who were forced to leave their little children and babies alone in the poor quarters they called home had to lock them in. There were cases where the little ones were tied to a table-leg from early morning until some member of the family came back briefly at noon to feed them.

Through the influence of Jane Addams, the terrible conditions in the sweatshops were exposed to the public. Provisions were drawn up for a new factory law in the State of Illinois, and in 1893 it was passed through the State Legislature. Now it was illegal for women to work more than eight hours a day or for factory work to be done by children under fourteen years of age. This was the beginning of many such movements, and of strikes, in which Jane Addams became supporter and sometimes even took the role of arbitrator. In some instances she brought heaps of criticism upon herself and Hull-House from those who disagreed with her; but always she stuck by her opinions and steadfastly held to her beliefs in the rights of the workers.

Because of her stand on labor and because of her work at the settlement, Jane Addams in the first ten years at Hull-House became a national figure. Hull-House became a model for other settlements that were springing up over the country, and social workers came there to study its methods and learn from its founder.

As many as a hundred volunteers a week gave of their time and energies in the steadily increasing activities at the settlement. The college extension classes grew to a size that required thirty-five college-trained men and women to instruct the eager young people who took the courses. Lectures held every Thursday evening, to begin with, grew to large proportions and eventually became the University Extension Courses of the University of Chicago. Classes in citizenship prepared the way for many of Chicago's immigrants to obtain their citizenship. A University of Chicago professor once wrote of Hull-House: "One of the chief functions of Hull-House has been to welcome the stranger, to smooth the path of the immigrant, to help adjust the foreign-born generations to American life."

The Juvenile Protective Association of Chicago started in 1909 to meet at Hull-House to conduct a clinic that tried to find the causes of juvenile delinquency. Always a subject close to Jane Addams's heart, the problems of children were a constant concern at Hull-House. The theory was practiced that to keep children busy was to keep them out of trouble with the law. Jane Addams was a firm believer in bringing out the creative abilities of children. To that end, there were at Hull-House a music school, classes in dancing and rhythm, a dramatic school, and the Hull-House Art School where boys and girls were taught to work with clay and colors.

One of the greatest sources of pleasure to young and old at Hull-House over the years was their vacation retreat called Bowen Country Club. This was a beautiful country estate of seventy-two acres along Lake Michigan which had been given to Hull-House by its very dear friend and staunch supporter Mrs. Joseph T. Bowen. Little children who had never before been outside the city were able to romp over its grounds, while elderly people enjoyed the flowers they had not seen since they left the old country. Besides the main house and dining-hall and cottages where the vacationers stayed, there was a boys' camp across the ravine among tall old trees. Though the activities of Hull-House make up an important part of the lives of the thousands who go there, many youngsters and oldsters, too, look upon Bowen Country Club as heaven.

Many honors came to Jane Addams during her busy years at Hull-House. Her never-failing faith in a future world of peace and her efforts toward that end were publicly rewarded in 1931 when she won the Nobel Peace Prize, awarded jointly to her and Dr. Nicholas Murray Butler. It was characteristic of Jane Addams that she donated her share of the prize money to the Women's International League for Peace and Freedom. She had founded this organization in 1915 and, first as President and then as Honorary President, she remained its staunch ally until her death. The same year she was given the Nobel Prize, she received from Bryn Mawr College a prize of five thousand dollars which has been awarded only at intervals to a woman of outstanding achievement. When Dr. Marion Parks, the President of Bryn Mawr, announced the award she said in part: "For the helpless, young and old, for the poor, the unlearned, the stranger, the despised, you have urged understanding and then justice."

The government of Greece, presenting her with a medal for her work at Hull-House among the Greek population of the city, called her "the greatest among modern women."

Jane Addams was always in demand as a public speaker. In spite of her very busy life she filled many engagements all over the country. Colleges awarded Jane Addams fourteen degrees. Her writings included many articles and several important books. But to Jane Addams her most important work was at Hull-House. It fulfilled the great objective of her life.

Just before her death on May 21, 1935, Jane Addams attended the twentieth anniversary meeting of her beloved International League in Washington. The words of Harold L. Ickes, then Secretary of the Interior, were a final and lasting tribute:

"Most of us have believed that neither race nor creed nor color should debar anyone from the full and free enjoyment of our American life. How few of us, however, have had the courage to live up to our professed principles! Be it said to her everlasting credit that Miss

Addams has. She does not talk about the Christian virtues; she practices them. . . . She is the truest American that I have ever known, and there has been none braver."

When Jane Addams threw open wide the doors of Hull-House, she also opened the doors of social settlements all over the land. The countless millions who have passed through these doors can all be grateful to her.

Lillian Wald: visiting nurse

It was a dreary, drizzly day in March, 1893. In an old building on Henry Street in New York City's "East Side" district, a young woman medical student was giving a lesson in bed-making to a group of women. Suddenly a little girl appeared, frightened and desperate, to ask help for her mother who was very ill. The sympathetic young instructor excused herself from her class, picked up the sheets she had been using in her demonstration and went with the child.

She was led through the dismal and dirty streets to an unbelievably filthy, crowded tenement house, typical of the time. She found her patient lying on rough planks which served as a bed, and there were several children in the room, half-dressed in rags and looking as though they had not eaten in a long while.

The young medical student went straight to work doing what she could for the mother, bathing her and putting clean linens on the bed, but she did not stop working until she also had the room as clean as possible. She washed the children and fed them with food she went out and bought herself. When, exhausted, she finally made her way home over the slimy, cobblestoned streets late that night, she knew what she had to do. She would give up her medical career and devote her life to nursing the sick who were in such desperate need of help right in their own homes.

The young woman was Lillian Wald and the decision she made that night was to have far-reaching results of which she had not the faintest conception at the time.

Lillian Wald was not a native New Yorker. She was born March 10, 1867, in Cincinnati, Ohio. The families of her parents, who were of Polish-German-Jewish ancestry, had come to this country in 1848. Unlike many other immigrants of this era, they had not been forced to leave their native land to avoid persecution, but because they thought that greater opportunities would be open to them in the United States.

Max Wald, Lillian's father, was a gentle person, kind and thoughtful, and happiest when surrounded by his family.

From her mother, Lillian inherited her trust in her fellow men. Minnie Wald was thought by some to be impractical because she believed completely in everybody's honesty. She enjoyed being surrounded by beautiful things in her home, and she was very generous to others. She loved books and believed in sharing them with her children. Her influence on her daughter's life could be seen later on, in the program Lillian Wald set up in her work with New York City's needy families.

When Lillian was a little girl her family moved to Rochester, where her father was engaged in the optical business. It must have been a happy childhood, for the children Julia, Alfred, Lillian and little Gus were brought up in an atmosphere of deep family love, and their grandfather Schwarz, or Favey as he was affectionately called, was a wonderful storyteller.

Lillian was educated in private schools that specialized in turning out young ladies equipped with all the social graces, which seems a rather strange background for a young girl who decided on nursing as a career. It came about in this manner.

After being turned down for admission to Vassar because she was too young, Lillian was visiting her older sister Julia, now Mrs. Charles P. Barry, at her summer home at the seashore. Julia had a new baby and the nurse assigned to her case was a Bellevue Hospital graduate. Lillian had never talked with a nurse before and was fascinated with all the information she got from her about the hospital training course and her experiences after graduation.

It seemed to Lillian that this completely different life would open up a whole new world! She was determined that nursing would be the career she would follow. Having persuaded her family that she was really serious in her determination, she went to New York Hospital for an interview with Miss Irene H. Sutcliffe, the director of nurses. Miss Sutcliffe recognized that this attractive and yet somewhat impulsive girl would be sympathetic and understanding and have the necessary qualities for a good nurse.

It was not easy for Lillian at first. In her later years, in speaking of her girlhood, she says she had been spoiled. In the strict discipline of hospital training, she lived in an atmosphere she had never known before, but she was as determined as she was high-spirited. Shocked at the poverty and suffering she saw among her patients, she knew she had found a way to help those less fortunate than herself. Her impulsiveness sometimes led her into trouble. Once, she raided the hospital icebox for food for a hungry patient. Another time she forgot to take a patient's temperature because she was so much more interested in cheering him up!

Nurses' training courses in those days lasted only eighteen months. So on March 31, 1891, Lillian Wald was graduated and shortly afterward she took her first nursing position, in an orphanage. There and then she made up her mind that if there was one thing she didn't like it was institutionalized care for children. She knew also that the discipline required of one who nursed in an institution was not for her. Doctors had more freedom. They were not bound down to routine as nurses were and there were many more opportunities open to them. So the next year she enrolled at the Women's Medical College in New York City.

Although it had been about forty years since Elizabeth Blackwell, the first woman doctor, had graduated from medical school, medicine was still a pioneer field for women to enter. Nevertheless, Lillian Wald decided it was right for her; but while she was a student at the Women's Medical College she was asked to conduct a class for immigrant women in home nursing in the old building on Henry Street. Her acceptance of the invitation led to the incident that was to change the course not only of her own life but of many others.

Overcrowded living conditions have always been a problem in large cities. In the New York City of 1893, conditions could not have been worse. There had been huge waves of immigration. First it had been the Irish, then the Germans, and now the Jewish and Italian immigrants were pouring in. Arriving full of hope for beginning a new life, they found living situations in America as bad if not worse than the ones they had left. There was not enough room for them and they were forced to live in buildings where a large family might have only one or two rooms. Because of the high rents, some were forced to take roomers besides, and there was never enough money to buy proper food or clothing. Crowded living quarters encouraged the spread of disease, but the unsanitary condition of the streets didn't help either. The city made no provision for garbage disposal in that area and refuse was flung into the streets to grow foul. The night Lillian Wald made up her mind to give up her medical career, she made another decision, too. She would find another nurse who shared her views and they would live together in the poor part of the city and be near those they wanted to help.

Having made up her mind, Miss Wald was not one to waste any time. She enlisted the help of a friend, Mary Brewster, and they set out to find a place to live. It was not easy. At first they lived at a settlement house with some young social workers. When they finally found a place of their own, it was at the top of five long flights of stairs, but it had an advantage very few places had—a bathroom.

It was not long before people around them began to accept the young nurses as their own kind. They inspired confidence by their concern over the sick and their willingness to be on call at any time and—what was most important—the fact that they never seemed to feel themselves above those they helped. They convinced everyone that they were sincerely grateful to be asked to be of service.

Because Miss Wald knew that the poor she wished to help had great respect for authority, she persuaded the president of the Board of Health of New York to permit her and Mary Brewster to wear a little badge that said: "Visiting Nurse. Under the Auspices of the Board of Health." Soon it was a common sight to see the two young nurses, dressed in blue, emerge from their house each morning carrying their little satchels complete with nursing equipment and start out on their rounds.

Although there were other nurses doing charitable work in the city, they were all employed by various religious organizations and were available only to special cases. Lillian Wald and Mary Brewster were truly the first visiting nurses whose services were not bound by race or creed. They were ready and anxious to serve all who needed them.

Their work didn't stop with nursing. They were increasingly aware of the education needed to get rid of the conditions that were causing so much sickness. They knew that somehow they must convince the authorities how necessary it was to clean up the streets, enforce quarantines and even provide jobs for those who needed them so desperately.

So many people began flocking to their rooms for help and advice that the girls realized they must have larger quarters. Also, money began to come in from various organizations to be spent at their discretion and more nurses asked to join their staff. There was more work to be done than time for doing it. But first of all they had to search for a new place.

They found it at 265 Henry Street—a whole house, where they could live and have classrooms and meeting rooms besides. At first their house was called the "Nurses' Settlement House," but they soon realized that with a sissy name like that they wouldn't have patronage from boys, so the house became the "Henry Street Settlement." To later generations the famous building was known as "the House on Henry Street."

As time went on, the work of the settlement house increased considerably and Lillian Wald was forced to give up some of her actual nursing duties and become director of the growing organization. One of her main concerns was the welfare of the nation's children. Little children were being allowed to work in factories long before they should have given up their schooling, and before they were physically able to do the work. When Theodore Roosevelt was President she secured an interview with him and presented her plan for forming a Children's Bureau.

She proposed an organization at the national level which would collect information concerning children's welfare and have it available to anyone who needed it. The President agreed with her, but although there was lots of pressure on Congress for such a law there was even more against it.

No legislation on this matter was passed for seven years, but in 1912 President Taft signed a law which created the Children's Bureau Lillian had suggested.

Lillian Wald never ceased in her fight to improve living conditions.

Just the creation of a Children's Bureau was not enough; there must be a wide public awareness of what was going on. At every opportunity she spoke on the subject before organizations. Soon she was being invited to appear before city, state and Federal boards with her facts, and because she was so persuasive, her influence began to be felt widely. Even though her national contacts with important persons increased, she never entirely gave up her work with individuals who called upon her for help. She had a telephone beside her bed and was always available for any emergency.

When Lillian Wald died in 1940 she had seen some of her dreams come true. The Visiting Nurse Association had spread over the country. The city was aware of its slums and was trying to do something about them. Although there would always be some, at least those in authority were unable to close their eyes to such conditions, as they had formerly. More playgrounds for children had been opened. The unsanitary condition of the streets was being corrected.

One of the reasons Lillian Wald was able to accomplish so much was that she had the ability to put herself in an unfortunate person's place. Her sympathy and understanding were outstanding and she had an unusual imagination. She not only saw what should be corrected; she could see how to do it. She was not afraid to champion unpopular projects, and she never considered herself. She was interested in only one thing—how she could help others.

Evangeline Booth and the Salvation Army

When Eva Booth was twelve years old she began preaching on street-corners in the slums of London. Standing on a drum so she would be tall enough for her audience to see her, she made people listen by the very sincerity of her words and her clear, ringing voice. Preaching came as naturally to Eva as talking, for all her young life she had been exposed to it. When, at the age of five, she had begun by preaching to her dolls, she was simply following the example of her father and mother, who were both preachers.

Eva Cory Booth (she later changed her name to Evangeline) was born on Christmas Day in 1865. The seventh of eight children, she was raised in a family that was one of the busiest in all England. Her father was General and Founder of the Salvation Army. Her mother, Catherine, divided her time between taking care of her large family and working with her husband at the Mission.

Eva's father, William Booth, had begun to preach on street-corners in the town of Nottingham at the age of seventeen. So engrossed was he in his plan to help the poor that he lived on almost nothing, saving what he could from his job in a pawnshop. When he decided that he had enough money, he moved to London and in 1878 opened up a mission in an old deserted mill. This was the beginning of the Salvation Army, and he was its General until his death.

Evangeline Booth learned much from her father. Of all the children, she was most like him in physical appearance. What was more significant, she had inherited his courage and determination and his ardent love of orderliness. At home, she had been schooled in punctuality, cleanliness and order. In a day when bathing was not considered important, a daily bath was required in the Booth household. No ashes were ever left on the hearth. Toys and books were always put back in place. Meals were served punctually and all the children were expected to be in their places at the proper time. The Mission was operated by General Booth on military lines, with officers who received promotion only when they deserved it. Evangeline was used to this kind of discipline and adhered to it all her life.

Mrs. Booth played an important part in the early years of the Salvation Army. She was very fond of music and taught the others to sing and play instruments. It was she who designed the dark blue uniform and big poke bonnet worn by all the women of the "Army." The sight of that uniform was to become a familiar one all over the world before Evangeline's life work was over. In the Booth family and in the Army women were considered the equal of men. Perhaps this was one reason why Evangeline never hesitated to take on any new responsibility, no matter how tremendous.

From the time she was in her teens, Evangeline went anywhere her father would have gone. Her slight figure with its dark blue uniform, blonde hair peeking out from beneath the poke bonnet that framed her determined face, was seen in dirty hovels, in filthy saloons and on the streets of the vilest slums in London. For the most part she went unharmed, but sometimes bottles were thrown at her or pails of water were dumped on her from upstairs windows of the tenements. It was not always the people who made it hard for her. On one occasion while she was conducting a service on the main street of Hackney, she was arrested by a policeman and taken to the police station. She was later released. But she was far too determined to give up. She had learned to play the accordion and she had a good singing voice. Soon the people were used to seeing her, and many came to listen to her when she preached.

One day a man well known in the British courts as a great orator and statesman heard her preach. John Bright went up to her and praised her. "You must take care of yourself," he said. "The world needs your like."

This was a truth that Evangeline was becoming more and more certain of. The world did need her. She resolved to let nothing deter her from the work she must do. When men came courting her she turned them down. She would devote her life to the Salvation Army.

Her abilities as a leader developed early in her life. After having proved herself in London she was sent by her father to Canada to become Field Commissioner of the Salvation Army there. She was only thirty-one years old. In 1898 she proved her theory that the Army could go anywhere to serve those who needed it. She sent a party of Salvationists out to the Alaskan gold fields to bring relief to the miners there and to preach the word of God to them.

In 1880 an English family by the name of Shirley wrote to General Booth and begged him to send Salvationists to the United States. And so the first contingent of the "Army" came to this country in the persons of Commissioner Railton and "seven female officers." A Philadelphia stable became the first Salvation Army Headquarters in the United States. Years later, Evangeline Booth wrote: "As from the stable in Bethlehem where Jesus was born . . . so from this stable in Philadelphia have come free dispensaries for the suffering poor; emergency and rescue homes for the unfortunate; relief depots supplying coal and blankets in winter, ice and milk for the babies in summer; hospitals for the sick; the poor man's church; the poor mother's meeting-room; the young girl's sewing-room; the working-man's club, and a place where the hounded, the sorrowing and the guilty can lay down their burden at the Saviour's feet and be free."

After eight years in Canada, Evangeline Booth took over the command in the United States. On the evening of December 6, 1904, she was given a tumultous welcome in Carnegie Hall, New York, by an enthusiastic crowd. Those who listened to her eloquent speech that night could not fail to recognize her qualities of leadership, her ability to "grow" with the Salvation Army in all that lay ahead.

A great deal did lie ahead for the Army. April, 1906, saw one of the worst disasters ever to strike the nation, the great earthquake and fire of San Francisco. The Salvation Army instantly rose to the occasion. Its San Francisco Headquarters had been wiped out, but relief was quick to come. At a meeting in Union Square in New York the initial sum of twelve thousand dollars was raised to begin the vast work of relief that was to be done by the organization. The quality and extent of the aid that was offered to the stricken people of San Francisco was a forerunner of the kind of wonderful action that people learned to expect from the Salvation Army at all times of disaster.

When the United States joined the Allied Forces in the First World War in 1917, the lassies of the Salvation Army accompanied the "doughboys" to the battlefields, serving them with coffee and doughnuts and cheering words. General Pershing saw to it that the uniforms of the many men and women Salvationists were made distinguishable by having them add special epaulettes to their uniforms. The soldiers called every woman worker "Sally," and Sally was everywhere, no matter how sloshy the mud and perilous the field. As a result of the magnificent work done by the Salvation Army, Evangeline Booth was decorated with the Distinguished Service Medal.

In 1934 Miss Booth was elected General of the Salvation Army, which made it necessary for her to go back to Headquarters in England. But before she left New York to accept this greatest of all her responsibilities, she was given a farewell in Madison Square Garden by a crowd of twenty thousand. Among the distinguished people in the audience were Attorney General Homer Cummings, representing President Roosevelt, and the mayor of New York. The ceremonies were broadcast by radio across the United States.

Evangeline Booth had been a tremendous success in the United States. She was a great orator, filling any hall in any city with eager listeners. When she went to Washington, D.C., to speak, men and women from the highest government posts went to hear her. Some said she could have been a famous actress. Her feeling for the dramatic and her keen wit were great assets in holding her audiences, and those who heard her speak were never likely to forget her.

The five years spent as General of the "Army" were busy ones. At the end of that time she relinquished the post and returned to America. When she died in 1950, she had lived to see the work begun in London by her father and a few other hardy souls develop into an army of nearly fourteen million workers, serving ninety-seven countries and territories over the world. Ten years after her death, the Salvation Army in the United States alone, active in all fifty states, had more than eighty-five hundred centers of operation. Army institutions included treatment centers, maternity homes and hospitals, camps, clubs for boys and girls, community recreation centers, U.S.O. and Red Shield Clubs for service men, mobile canteens and numerous family service bureaus. Even Evangeline Booth with all her insight and imagination could not have foretold such a future.

There were two things she firmly believed in all her life. The first was service. "Salvationists have little use for a Christian who is of no use to the community!" she said. The second was the right to happiness of all classes of people. When referring to the Declaration of Independence, she said, "That immortal instrument of aspiration belongs no longer to one nation. It is among the charters of mankind. Everywhere the community is recognizing that the pursuit of happiness must be included among the unalienable rights of all people."

part III
CARING FOR THOSE IN NEED

CARING FOR THOSE IN NEED

*The highest of distinctions
is service to others.*

—GEORGE VI OF ENGLAND

Recently, the American Association for the United Nations estimated that one half of mankind still goes to bed hungry. Over the years many organizations have been formed to care for these people who are in desperate need. Some of them have been of local origin, some national and some international. They have been created to take care of specific situations of short duration and also to take care of those people whose need continues indefinitely.

Six of these organizations are discussed in the following chapter. The American Relief Administration no longer exists but the work it did was so important that it will always be remembered as one of the great humanitarian efforts in history. Assistance to refugees is now administered by the United Nations. The Red Cross, the American Friends Service Committee, CARE and MEDICO continue to benefit mankind.

The American Relief Administration
of World War I

Almost everyone at some time or other in his life becomes conscious of the plight of people in the world who are hungry and homeless. During the years just following World War I, Americans were reminded often of such situations. Although they might have had to deprive themselves of certain foods and comforts during the war, they did not have to live in a country which had been overrun by enemy soldiers, where homes were destroyed and where food was scarce.

Pictures and articles appeared in newspapers and magazines that touched Americans deeply. One picture had no story accompanying it, nor did it need one. Its caption simply said, "His daddy is not coming back." It was a photograph of some American doughboys sharing their food with a little orphaned French boy. The child's coat, obviously intended for an older boy, hangs nearly to his ankles. His shoes, many sizes too large, look as though they will soon fall to pieces. His whole attitude is one of complete dejection.

But our allies were not the only ones in trouble. Another picture was taken in Berlin. It too, has no story with it. Several women, advanced in years, leaning on canes for support, are searching for bits of food to eat among the rubbish at the city garbage dump.

Whether help was needed for our allies or our former enemies, Americans recognized human misery when they saw it and dug deep into their pockets to provide funds for food supplies and medical aid.

This post-war situation was not the first time Americans had been asked to help feed the hungry people of Europe. Relief had started back in 1914 when the European War first broke out.

One of the first war moves England made against her enemy, Germany, was a blockade of all German shipping, and she successfully bottled up the German fleet. To retaliate for this, the Germans, who were occupying Belgium in their drive toward France, placed a strict food blockade on that little country.

The situation reached a stalemate. The British refused to lift their blockade because they were trying to starve Germany into submission. They also refused to allow any food to be taken into Belgium for fear the Germans would seize it and use it for themselves.

The Germans, short of food, refused to share any of theirs with the Belgians and the Belgians were the innocent victims caught in the middle.

Millard K. Shaler, an American mining engineer living in Brussels, was determined to do something about the situation. He managed to get to London and immediately asked help of another American mining engineer. Herbert Hoover, at that time living in London, had already earned a reputation for such work.

At the beginning of the war, event had followed event so rapidly that about ten thousand American tourists were trapped in Europe when fighting began. They had flocked to London and besieged Mr. Page, the American Ambassador, to secure passage home for them. But war preparations were under way and already the ships were being converted for the use of troops.

Not only was transportation a problem but food was scarce in London because of the sudden increase in population.

The American Ambassador had finally turned to one of his countrymen for help. Herbert Hoover was a man with a reputation for efficiency and accomplishment. Within a few days he had an organization established which managed to provide the frantic tourists with funds and, eventually, transportation home.

When Mr. Shaler came to see Hoover about helping the Belgians, they both talked the situation over with Ambassador Page. Together they decided to set up an organization for Belgian relief, and Hoover was asked to take charge. Because of the pressing need of the Belgians it was necessary that there be no delay. Soon the organization which had started as a charity grew to such proportions that it was functioning as a government.

The allies and the Germans both recognized the new organization, and its representatives were allowed to pass freely from country to country. American ships were used to transport food from the United States and carried banners with "Belgian Relief Commission" emblazoned on them. The organization guaranteed that it would carry nothing but food and clothing and for some time the ships were unmolested by German submarines. At that time everyone thought the organization was a temporary measure, as the war would probably be over in eight months. No one dreamed that it would last four years.

One of Belgium's problems was that her industries had completely collapsed and citizens had no way of earning money. Prices had soared so high that few people could afford to purchase what little food there was, which meant that practically a whole nation had to be fed.

Soup kitchens were set up everywhere and it was a common sight to see children carrying soup home in little buckets to those who were unable to go to the kitchens themselves. The Americans had invented a special cracker which contained all the chemicals a growing child needs in his diet. In addition to the soup, each child received one of the crackers daily. Americans contributed generously to this relief fund for people caught up in a war they had no part in making.

Then, in 1917, America entered the war and food became a problem at home. Everyone was urged to conserve it and posters with the slogan, "Food will win the war," were seen everywhere. Once again Herbert Hoover was called upon, and President Woodrow Wilson appointed him head of the Food Administration.

When the war ended, the food problem was still the greatest one to be solved. Not only were the Allies in desperate need but there were the neutral nations, the liberated countries and the enemy countries. All together there were twenty-nine countries with about 110,-000,000 people. And added to these was the new nation of Soviet Russia which had a population of about 170,000,000.

Something had to be done, and done quickly. Not only was much farm land ravaged by war, but there was a lack of farm equipment, as all factories had been converted to war use.

Once more, America stretched forth a helping hand. The newly named American Relief Administration, under the leadership of Herbert Hoover, supervised agricultural production and arranged for the rationing of food.

Literally millions of children throughout Europe were undernourished or diseased. Many of them were orphans. In each community a committee of leading citizens was formed to assist the American Relief Administration and undertake the work of caring for the young. Soon children were being supplied three meals a day, clothing was provided and there was medical attention for those who needed it.

By September, 1919, things were pretty much under control and it was decided that the time had come to withdraw American workers from Europe. The countries were recovering from their war years. Factories were being rebuilt to produce their own equipment. The land, recently the scene of battles, was being reclaimed to raise food. People whose lives had been disrupted by the horrors of war were beginning to live normally again.

But the work of the American Relief Administration should not be forgotten. It saved millions of persons from starvation and it restored millions of little children to health.

World refugees and the Nansen Passports

Visitors to the first assembly of the League of Nations in Geneva, Switzerland, in 1920 must have paused to look with admiration and respect at one of the delegates. He was a tall man with the build of an athlete, who gave the impression of great strength. His hair was snow-white and he had a flowing white mustache. On his head he usually wore a wide-brimmed hat tilted up on one side at a rather jaunty angle. No one had to ask who this outstanding-looking person was, for he was a familiar figure all over the world—not because he was a well-known diplomat, but because he had gained considerable fame as an Arctic explorer. He was Fridtjof Nansen, head of the Norwegian delegation to the League of Nations.

The European War, or World War I as it was later known, was over. The League of Nations was trying to create a peaceful world out of one which had suffered widespread destruction.

One problem that needed to be solved immediately was that of the prisoners-of-war still scattered in prison camps all over Europe. All of them were hungry and most of them were sick. There seemed to be no place for most of them to go when they were released or, if there was a place, no means to get them there.

Confusion reigned everywhere. Some of the nations that had placed the men in prison didn't even exist as separate countries after the peace treaty was signed. Newly created countries disclaimed responsibility for the prisoners within their boundaries. In Russia this was the chief difficulty. The Revolution had taken place while the war was still going on. The new Soviet government was having too much trouble getting organized after overthrowing the Czarist regime to have any thought for prisoners taken during the early war years.

Besides the war prisoners, there was the overwhelming problem of refugees. Most of these had fled their homelands because of political revolutions. Many of them had had a great deal of wealth and were untrained in any kind of profession and unequipped to earn a living. Poland, Turkey and Germany were filled with such people.

The League of Nations decided that the only way out of all this chaos was to appoint one efficient person to form his own organization and get relief to the prisoners and refugees as soon as possible. Its choice for the job was Fridtjof Nansen.

Nansen knew a great deal about organization and he had experienced enough hardships himself to appreciate what they meant. He was born on October 10, 1861, near what is now Oslo, Norway. In 1882, when he had taken his first trip to the Arctic on a sealing vessel, he had decided to organize an expedition to cross Greenland. He and six others made that trip and it took them a year. Four years later, in the midsummer of 1893, he and his companions set forth on a Polar expedition in their ship the *Fram*. For two years they slowly took their way through icy seas. After reaching a point as far north as they could travel in their ship, Nansen and a chosen companion left their comrades and set out by dog sledge and skis. On April 8, 1895, they reached a point farther north than any human being had been before.

Nansen was a great scientist. Besides his interest in the Arctic, he was absorbed in the study of oceanography. His writings about it were a great contribution to the subject. He was a statesman, too, and was one of the leaders in bringing about the separation of Norway and

Sweden. When Norway became a separate monarchy he was appointed its first Minister to England.

With all this varied experience, it is little wonder that the League of Nations chose him for the tremendous task of taking care of the refugees. He was named High Commissioner and placed in complete charge of the project.

To secure the release of the prisoners in Russia and to get them transported out of the country, it was of course necessary for Nansen to work with the Soviet officials. The League of Nations had refused to recognize the new Soviet government and therefore the Russian leaders did not recognize the League as an organization with which they could work; but they did have respect for Nansen and agreed to cooperate with him as an individual.

As a result of this situation, the Nansen Relief Organization, completely separated from the League, was created. It received its financial aid at first mostly from the International Red Cross and from several National Red Cross organizations. Later on, through the personal efforts of Nansen, who traveled widely making public appeals in behalf of the refugees and prisoners, it received funds from private sources.

One of the first difficulties Nansen had to face was transporting the refugees and prisoners from one country to another. No country claimed them; none was willing to issue them passports.

In 1922, in order to get the homeless persons settled in countries where they could work and make permanent homes, Nansen called together a convention in Geneva and offered a proposition. He suggested that his office issue to each refugee a passport and that the nations recognize it as such. The passport would be good for a year and could be renewed yearly on the payment of what would be equal to a dollar in our money. The nations agreed to his plan, and so came into being the Nansen Passports.

The passport has a picture of Nansen in the center. Over it are these words:

Societé—Des—Nations
Haut Commissariat Pour Les Refugiés

and, underneath his portrait, followed by the date of issuance:

Resolution
De
Genève

The tragedy that Nansen found in country after country was almost overwhelming. War had brought famine and thousands were starving. Added to this, disease was spreading, as there were practically no medical supplies. Nansen and Herbert Hoover, who was in charge of the International Relief Organization, worked together trying to stem a wave of epidemics.

But 1922 brought more trouble, this time in Asia Minor between Greece and Turkey. The Greeks and Armenians in Asia Minor, knowing their lives were in danger from the Turks, fled into Greece. Greece was not able to cope with the million or so refugees suddenly crowding into her cities and towns, and she appealed to the League for aid. Once again the League turned over to Nansen the problem of caring for the homeless persons. Through his efforts new villages were founded and, with the help of a loan to Greece from the League of Nations, 1,250,000 refugees were settled in Greece.

In December of that same year, Fridtjof Nansen was awarded the Nobel Peace Prize in recognition of the great humanitarian work he had performed. He used part of his prize money as a contribution to help instruct the Russian peasants in modern agricultural methods, and gave the rest to the fund for Greek refugees.

Although Fridtjof Nansen died in 1930, the work that he had started was continued in his name. In 1931, the League of Nations established, for a seven-year period, the Nansen International Office for Refugees.

During the depression of the nineteen thirties, it became increasingly difficult for refugees to find employment. Even the charitable private organizations, operating under reduced funds, were not able to help as much as they had formerly. So that displaced persons would have some legal protection, the League in 1933 issued a Nansen Identity Certificate that would ensure their rights to residence and employment.

But the refugee problem never seemed to be solved. In 1938, many persons were fleeing Nazi Germany and by the end of World War II, the problem was greater than ever. Now, instead of the League of Nations, there was a new organization, the United Nations, to assume the responsibility.

The first organization set up by the United Nations immediately after World War II was the Relief and Rehabilitation Administration (UNRRA). In 1946, this was supplanted by the International Relief Organization (IRO). In December 1950, the office of the United Nations High Commissioner for Refugees was established. Its purpose is to help coordinate the work relating to refugees in those countries which admit them.

On July 28, 1951, a special Convention on the Status of Refugees approved the idea of replacing the Nansen Passport with a travel document of its own, but the Convention did not come into force until April 22, 1954. Until that time the Nansen Passport continued to be issued to Russian, Armenian and similar refugees in Belgium, France, Switzerland and the United Kingdom, and to Russian and Armenian refugees in Greece. A special certificate of identity was issued in Ireland and Italy.

By 1961, seven countries, Belgium, France, Greece, Ireland, Italy, Switzerland and the United Kingdom were issuing the Convention travel document to those refugees whose problems had not been solved by naturalization, repatriation or death.

Although many years have passed since 1921, Fridtjof Nansen's work will not be forgotten. Indeed, his name is perpetuated in the Nansen Medal bestowed on those whose work with refugees is outstanding. And those who receive it believe as Nansen did that peace depends on the feeling of brotherhood in the hearts of men.

The story of the Red Cross

ITS HISTORY

Many great organizations have been started by the efforts of just one person. None has been so far-reaching and has brought relief to so many millions as that which was started through the deep concern of a single individual in Europe, something over a hundred years ago. The year was 1859 and the man was Henri Dunant, a Swiss who was traveling in Italy when the Battle of Solferino took place. The war was between the France of Napoleon III and Austria, over the political future of Italy. The bitter battle, which brought about the defeat of Austria, was fought on a hot June day and the wounded soldiers of both sides lay in agony on the battlefield, unattended. It was this sight that struck at the heart of M. Dunant. He enlisted what help he could get from a nearby village, and the wounded were dragged out of the blazing sun to shelter, and given water and whatever medical aid could be administered.

But the episode did not stop there. It had set M. Dunant to thinking. He wrote a book about his experience and then traveled all over Europe talking about his idea for forming volunteer groups to care for the war-wounded. His efforts were rewarded when a conference met in Geneva in 1863 to discuss forming volunteer aid societies in every country. There the International Red Cross was born. The Red Cross was to become a symbol of humanitarian relief around the world. Its name was chosen to honor Henri Dunant and his native Swiss flag, and the Red Cross on a white ground was the Swiss flag reversed.

The following year there was another meeting in Geneva. This time thirty-six delegates from eighteen nations met and the Geneva Convention was drawn up—the first treaty "to assure protection to wounded soldiers and the personnel caring for them." From that beginning the Geneva Convention has grown into the eighty-four Red Cross Societies it comprises today.

Henri Dunant had suggested from the first that the victims of the disasters of peacetime were as much in need of help as the wounded on the battlefield. Gradually, in several European countries, peacetime emergency needs were met by Red Cross societies, but they functioned mostly in time of war.

In our own country at this time the Civil War was being fought. Now it is hard to picture the United States without the Red Cross. But, even though many people during the war urged our nation to join the Geneva Convention, Congress refused, because there was still a very strong feeling against alliances with other nations. And so the

United States Sanitary Commission did what it could to care for the wounded on the battlefields and in the hospitals.

After the war was over many sincere people worked to get the government to join the Geneva Convention of Red Cross Societies. Foremost among these was Clara Barton.

Clara Barton, a teacher from Massachusetts, had resigned her position to care for the sick and wounded soldiers in the Civil War. During the Franco-German War she went to Europe and worked with the International Red Cross. Then, returning to the United States, she threw all her efforts into a campaign to establish an American Red Cross. In 1882 the United States became a part of the Geneva Convention of Red Cross Societies, the thirty-second nation to become a member. Clara Barton was first President of the American Red Cross and served until 1904.

The Spanish-American War of 1898 gave the American Red Cross its first experience in wartime service. Its invaluable assistance led to the government's granting the Red Cross its first charter, making it the official agency for welfare work with the armed forces of the nation. The charter named the organization the official agency for disaster preparedness and relief. The Spanish-American War saw the Red Cross grow in size and extent of services. It first extended its aid beyond the boundaries of the United States when a group headed by Clara Barton went to Cuba to give assistance and distribute hospital supplies and food.

A new charter formed in 1905 is the same one under which the present-day Red Cross operates. Several new services were started, among them the program for training volunteer workers. This feature of Red Cross work by volunteers has become the backbone of the organization as we know it today.

During World War I, the American Red Cross grew and expanded rapidly. Even before the United States had entered the war, hospital units and supplies had been sent to the warring countries of Europe. After our entry into the war, a War Council was formed in the United States to direct the American Red Cross in its war effort. Everywhere throughout the country, chapters were being formed, with volunteers making millions of surgical dressings, bandages and garments, and packing comfort kits and other supplies. These were distributed to hospitals, to men in the armed forces and to the civilians of war-torn countries. Everywhere, Red Cross canteens sprang up to bring cheer to servicemen at their home bases, at their points of embarkation and at posts overseas. Ambulance sections were supplied and staffed by the Red Cross, while the Red Cross nurse became a familiar and welcome sight to the wounded and sick. Through the operation of Home Service, a link was formed between servicemen and their families at home. Aside from the work done with the armed forces, thousands of refugees overseas were cared for in France, Italy, Serbia, Rumania and Russia.

It was during World War I that the American Junior Red Cross was founded by proclamation of President Wilson. This gave the school children throughout America an opportunity to contribute to the war effort.

When at last the war was over, the Red Cross carried on its work with veterans by helping them to become rehabilitated, offering them emergency financial assistance and helping them to claim government benefits due them. Their hospital work continued, too, for now there were veterans' hospitals where Red Cross workers were badly needed. Many Red Cross nurses who were returning from overseas found they were needed as rural public health nurses, or instructors in home nursing classes which were being conducted in all local chapters. These classes, as well as those in first aid and water safety, were very popular with the public.

For five years after World War I, the American Red Cross continued its work overseas. It operated public health hospitals and clinics, established orphanages for children who were war victims, and maintained many camps for refugees. It also distributed food, clothing and medical supplies in the war-torn countries of Europe. But the load was too great to be continued by one national organization, and because of the need, the League of Red Cross Societies came into being. It is this League that, since 1919, has correlated the work of Red Cross Societies around the world.

After the war the American Red Cross was kept busy taking care of distress areas that were ravaged by hurricanes in Florida, floods in Mississippi and droughts in the West. During the depression of the thirties, the Red Cross was besieged by requests for help from many destitute people. Among these were farmers to whom the Red Cross distributed eighty-five million bushels of wheat and 844,000 bales of cotton which had been turned over to that agency by the government from surplus stocks. The Red Cross made the wheat into flour and turned the cotton into blankets and materials that were made into clothing. Five million families benefited from this program.

When the U.S. Government took over the relief of victims of the depression, Red Cross was again able to concentrate on its regular programs. The floods of 1936 in the Ohio Valley and New England, followed by tornadoes in the South, gave the nation ample proof of what Red Cross aid meant to millions of people in times of disaster. Rebuilding and refurnishing homes and supplying medical aid and nursing care to the disaster victims required the work of one thousand case workers for more than six months in the Ohio Valley and New England areas alone.

In 1939, when war again came to Europe, the American Red Cross resumed its operations in European countries. After the fall of France, programs in England and unoccupied France were intensified. And after Pearl Harbor the Red Cross again served as in World War I, but on a much wider scale. It served in countries all over the globe. Wherever American servicemen were, at home or overseas, there was the Red Cross. Ninety per cent of the nurses who served with the armed forces were recruited by the Red Cross. American Red Cross field directors remained with the units assigned to them while they trained in the United States and then went overseas with them, regardless of their destination. This meant that field directors were stationed in virtually every corner of the earth, from the Aleutian Islands to Dakar; in China, India and Iran; on tiny islands of the South Pacific; as far north as Iceland and as far south as New Zealand.

A new service was begun by Red Cross during World War II which was responsible for saving thousands of lives. This was the blood-donor program. During the war period more than thirteen million pints of blood were collected for treating the wounded.

The extent of the American Red Cross program during World War II can hardly be imagined. Some idea of its scope and benefits can be imagined from the fact that its expenditures from July 1, 1939, to June 30, 1946, were $732 million. In addition, there was the contribution of countless millions of hours of service given by volunteer adults and children in the war effort.

The post-war program of the Red Cross again was gigantic. This time, however, the work overseas was carried on in cooperation with the League of Red Cross Societies. The two chief problems were to help the Red Cross Societies of the war-torn countries to get back in operation so they could help their own people and to provide the basic supplies they would need to carry out their programs.

The American Junior Red Cross made large contributions in the aid that was sent overseas. They packed numerous educational gift boxes and sent school supplies, clothing and other useful articles to children whose ravaged countries were destitute of such things.

The blood-donor program was dropped for a time, but in 1947 it was re-established at the request of doctors and hospitals throughout the United States. The Blood-Bank program, which continues today, became the first civilian blood program on a national scale in history.

During the Korean War all American Red Cross programs expanded to meet the needs of veterans and their families.

THE RED CROSS TODAY

Work overseas continues with the Armies of Occupation stationed in Europe and the Far East. Chapters have been formed in most of these places by American civilians to serve the veterans and their families.

But today the American Red Cross emphasizes peacetime service with flexible programs that can be expanded in times of emergency. Its objectives are to help the American family to solve the problems that arise from military service, to recover from the effects of storms, floods, fire and other peacetime disasters, to obtain blood needed for surgery and in illness, and to lead families to healthier and safer lives through the various Red Cross programs.

The American Red Cross is quick to pay tribute to its vast numbers of volunteers and the work accomplished by them. It is estimated that there are 155 volunteers to every one on the professional staff— a total of two million people in the thirty-six hundred local chapters who every year give of their time and talents to Red Cross.

Large numbers of Red Cross workers do volunteer work in veterans' hospitals. Among these are groups of men, many of them retired and eager to be of service. An increasing number of high school and college students also help with the veterans, many of whom are being rehabilitated and are in particular need of companionship and encouragement. Their contacts with outside volunteers are bright spots in their lives at the hospitals.

Nursing aides are taught by the Red Cross to care for the sick and injured, and an increasing number of them work with older citizens in nursing homes for the aged. Many young people of sixteen or older take the forty-hour course required to equip them to work as volunteer nurse's aides in hospitals. Another valuable assistance to the Red Cross is the large number of professional nurses who contribute their time to training the aides, giving courses in mother and baby care, and assisting in many other places where trained help is essential.

The many phases of work done at Red Cross headquarters give every interested individual an opportunity to find the particular kind of volunteer work for which he or she is most suited. Nurses' aides, Gray Ladies, Gray Men, staff aides, social welfare aides, and workers in Canteen, Arts and Skills, Motor, and Production Services—the field is wide and the need for the volunteer's services great.

Red Cross volunteer work by young people has grown steadily since it began with Junior Red Cross during World War I. Thousands of high school and college students have learned to perform many different kinds of services for their community through Red Cross training. Aside from their duties as Junior Aides in hospitals, they have learned to assist with recreation in children's wards, and to present dramatic and musical entertainment. In home economics and industrial and fine arts classes they have learned to make articles for the children and other patients of hospitals and other institutions. They have served on speakers' bureaus and at blood-donor centers and have been trained to assist in practically every branch of Red Cross services. They have also been trained to provide voluntary service for the armed forces and for military and veterans' hospitals. They have been able to contribute to world fellowship and good will through the international programs provided by the Red Cross. One such program is the High School Chest Program. Since it began in 1948, thirty-two countries where schools have been affected by disasters have received these chests from American school children. Another communication the American Junior Red Cross members have with children of other Red Cross societies is provided through the International Album Program. Since 1921, albums describing the American way of life have been prepared in school classes and sent abroad to members of Red Cross societies in other countries on an exchange program, so that American children, in turn, learn of the life of young people in other parts of the world.

Recently a new program has been started to provide international contacts for Junior Red Cross and high school members. In the summer of 1960, thirty-three high school members from Red Cross chapters in twenty states and Puerto Rico went abroad as guests of other Red Cross societies. One group visited five European countries; another attended a study center in England and visited Ireland. Another group visited the Scandinavian countries, and still others went to South America. In one recent summer, twenty-seven members visited countries in Latin America, while thirteen young representatives of the Chilean Red Cross came to visit the United States. An even larger exchange program is being planned for future years. Known as Vista (Visit of International Students to America), it is a combined study-travel-visit program to give young people an opportunity to know and understand each other.

In studying the history and the work of Red Cross it is easy to see that its volunteers, including school children of Junior Red Cross, High School and College members, housewives and businessmen, professional people and the retired, all have created this magnificent institution. The red cross on its field of white is familiar to all as a symbol of service. It represents a channel through which human beings can express their desire to help each other. The Red Cross is living proof that brotherhood is not dead in the world.

The American Friends Service Committee

Let us then try what Love will do.—WILLIAM PENN

It was on April 30, 1917, soon after the United States had declared war against Germany, that fourteen members of the American Society of Friends met in a small room in Philadelphia for a conference. They knew that men would be drafted for military service immediately, but they knew too that many of the young men of their faith, following the principles of quakerism, would refuse to bear arms. With those of some other religions with similar beliefs, they would be classed as conscientious objectors. The men at the meeting were deeply concerned, for they also knew that their young people would be eager to take active and useful parts in the war program short of combat duty. To fill this need, and to give aid to the civilians in war zones who would be in dire need of help, the American Friends Service Committee was founded. They made the following declaration of purpose: "We are united in expressing our love for our country and our desire to serve her loyally. We offer ourselves to the Government of the United States in any constructive work in which we can conscientiously serve humanity."

The new Service Committee was successor to the former Friends National Peace Committee which had functioned before the war. Now a whole new program was necessary. To start it, one hundred young men took part in a training period at Haverford College in preparation for work overseas. They studied carpentry (for reconstructing bombed-out homes), automotive engineering (for driving trucks and ambulances), medical aid (for treating the injured), and French (for communicating with French natives). In the meantime the office of the AFSC was very busy indeed, dealing with draft boards for releases, securing passports and arranging sailings to transport the workers overseas. During the war this work of training men and sending them abroad continued, while at the front and in the war-torn villages of France the members of the AFSC served in many ways. After the war was over they stayed on to help with the relief and rehabilitation work. At the request of the American Relief Administration they took charge of feeding the hungry children of Germany. They did reconstruction work in France, Poland and Russia, living with the villagers and lending them courage and confidence. One worker in France wrote home, "The reason we wanted to mend houses was that it gave us a chance to try to mend hearts."

Relief and reconstruction have been major services of the AFSC ever since it was first established. Since 1917, a succession of emergencies have presented opportunities for service in more than fifty countries. These have ranged from such projects as feeding more than a million German children in 1921; giving relief to families of North Carolina strike victims in 1929; rehabilitating the people of Finland after the second World War; feeding, clothing and setting up schools for Arab refugees in the Israeli war; distributing supplies to thousands of Hungarian refugees who escaped to Vienna during the Hungarian uprising of 1956.

Because of the impartiality of the Friends, their help has been welcomed in many areas where other groups could not go. Thus they were able to give medical aid on both sides of the battle lines in the Chinese Civil War, rescue both Hindus and Moslems in the India partition, and help both Jews and Arabs in Egypt.

After relief has been given to the suffering, AFSC has always concerned itself with human relations and human needs. In stricken areas it has developed neighborhood centers and schools.

One of its projects has been to help communities to adjust to changes that have been difficult for the people to meet. In the United States, when coal mines closed down during the depression, AFSC workers gave the people of the stricken communities a whole new outlook by teaching them to make furniture and build up a new industry. A different kind of adjustment, but one that helped the people to meet the change that came to their area, was made in villages of India. In 1957, when the vast new Hirakud Dam was completed, the people of that region were ready to use the irrigation and electric power resources because of the training that had been given them by AFSC. The villagers of Orissa expressed their pride in what they could now accomplish. One of them said, "You see, we now have a little more courage to do the things we never dreamed we could do before."

Community projects such as this have gone on in places throughout the world. The Service Committee has helped isolated villages in Italy with agricultural projects, clinics, work shops and literacy classes. Loans and housing for destitute widows in Kunsan, Korea, have helped them back to independence. Classes in language, sewing crafts and other subjects have been conducted in villages in Mexico, along with rural development projects there and in El Salvador. In Hong Kong the Service Committee conducts a day nursery for children of Chinese refugee mothers, while in Tunisia and Morocco, Algerian refugees attend classes where they learn knitting, machine sewing, carpentering and other skills. The AFSC has a firm belief that people of different backgrounds can become unified in their community. A neighborhood center in Acre, Israel, where Jews, Arabs and Christians used the baby clinic, attended craft classes and social functions together and shared their religious holidays, is now under local sponsorship.

Community work in our own country is stressed in areas where there is racial tension. From working with those who have housing problems in Philadelphia to helping people on Indian reservations, the projects continue. The Community Relations Division has an active program in the South, where the objectives are peaceful integration of public schools, equal employment opportunity and job advancement based on merit in business and industry.

Young "work campers" are active in many programs. A typical example of the accomplishments of these small groups is the work done by eighteen work campers in one summer on the Hoopa Indian Reservation in Northern California, where they cleared a dam and laid water pipes to bring in a supply of fresh mountain water. Twelve hundred young people, that same year, in small groups, worked in hospitals and industries and spent their weekends trying to improve conditions in the blighted neighborhoods to which they were assigned. In carrying out these projects the AFSC demonstrates again that love and service go hand in hand to unify a community.

Although the American Friends Service Committee was begun in wartime, its chief concern has always been to build for peace. A stand for peace is at the root of the Quaker religion, which refuses to sanction war or violence of any kind. But the Religious Society of Friends has cooperated with the government in times of war by serving in other ways than bearing arms, and its stand has always been respected by the government. In all its efforts in wartime and in reconstruction work afterward, the AFSC has never for a moment lost sight of its hopes for a peaceful world.

The peace work of the Committee has brought it into contact with the government at the policy-making level, as well as with leaders of communities and with citizens who have been perplexed by problems of peace and war. Beginning in 1930, Institutes of International Relations have been held annually at which more than two thousand people meet to discuss their problems. At these Institutes, people from all walks of life including churchmen, educators, community leaders and concerned citizens plan new approaches to advancing the movement for peace.

The Committee has long advocated talks between nations at all levels. It works closely with the United Nations and has opportunities for informal sessions with U.N. personnel and diplomats from the various member nations.

High School and college students hold their own institutes where they discuss world affairs and what can be done by their own groups to help in promoting peace. In a recent year AFSC sponsored nineteen summer institutes and camps. Among these were the camp at Lake Winnipesaukee, New Hampshire, where four hundred young people met; another group of four hundred at Houston, Texas; three hundred and fifty at the Middle Atlantic Region's Retreat in the Pocono Mountains of Pennsylvania; and a combined meeting of the Pacific Southwest and Northern California Regional Offices at Camp Sierra.

A new opportunity for young people is VISA (Voluntary International Service Assignments). It is exactly what its name implies and is the outgrowth of many requests from young people for longer-term assignments at working with young people of other countries. The VISA volunteers work on governmental and private agency projects where they learn the languages of the countries and share their knowledge and skills with the people they are visiting. By living, working and learning in places where the people's backgrounds are different from their own, they are able to demonstrate friendship and further the cause of peace. VISA volunteers are working in India, Pakistan, France, Germany, Tanganyika, Haiti, Guatemala, Morocco, Tunisia and the United States.

All ages of school children are reached by the Service Committee through its educational materials, prepared by its Children's Program staff. Brotherhood is emphasized by means of a variety of Service projects at home and abroad. More than two hundred American and European schools are linked through the School Affiliation Service. Not only letters and gifts are exchanged, but students and teachers as well. This practice bears out the principle that to know each other is to understand each other, and understanding brings love.

The peace-making policy of the AFSC has been more concerned with the prevention of war and strife than with picking up the pieces afterward. Its continuous efforts for peace have not gone unrecognized in the world. In 1947 the American Friends Service Committee and the British Friends Service Council were awarded jointly the Nobel Peace Prize.

William Penn, the most famous Quaker of all, once wrote these words: "Let us then try what Love will do: for if men did once see we love them, we should soon find they would not harm us."

The American Friends Service Committee works on that principle.

CARE and MEDICO:

gifts from the American people

CARE

An American newsman was making a trip through Central and South America. One day he stopped in Bogota, Colombia, to visit the CARE mission and see how it operated. The director of the mission took him to a school where CARE was providing needed food for the children. This school bore little resemblance to the modern American school with its latest educational equipment. Indeed, it had no equipment at all. Some of the classrooms had neither desks nor chairs and the children either had to stand or sit on the floor. There, in a dirt-floor courtyard, the newsman saw little children lined up for their daily ration of a cup of milk and a large bun. Most of the children didn't look very clean. Their clothes and even their faces were dirty. "Angels with dirty faces," he later called them. But they were friendly and happy to meet the American visitor.

The mission director explained that the milk and buns the children were receiving were probably the only bit of real nourishment in their diet. As the American watched, one little girl took a bite of her bun and then quickly put the rest in her pocket. She came from a family of eleven children and probably there was someone at home hungrier than she. After all, she had just had a cup of milk! Most of these children came to school without breakfast and this midmorning snack was the high point of their day.

It's a little hard for people living in a country where food is plentiful and where sometimes one gets a stomach-ache from overeating to realize what it must be like to get one from hunger. But that is what happens in many countries. In fact, it has been estimated that two-thirds of the people on earth don't have enough to eat. Besides being hungry, many of them are sick. Many have malaria or tuberculosis, or suffer from trachoma, the dread eye infection that causes blindness if it's not properly treated. It is to help people like these and to relieve some of the suffering caused by hunger and disease that CARE came into being.

In November, 1945, CARE (Cooperative for American Relief Everywhere) was organized to help the European nations that had been ravaged by war. Many Americans were anxious to help relatives and friends living in those countries but there was no reliable organization to see that aid would reach the persons who needed it. A number of welfare agencies, including religious, welfare, labor, nationality aid groups and service clubs, banded together to form an organization and set up a relief aid program.

At the present time CARE has expanded beyond its war relief to such a degree that it operates in thirty-two countries all over the world. It provides food, textiles and self-help tool packages, as well as medical and educational supplies to those in need. Food packages have always been an important part of the program but a great deal of emphasis is now being placed on self-help. Seed packages are sent so people can raise their own food. Plows are provided so farmers can make better use of their land. Cement and lumber help furnish better housing. Dental and hospital equipment go where needed. Books and other educational materials are sent to schools from elementary to university levels.

Because CARE has grown to be such a large organization it has been set up to work as efficiently as possible. It buys its supplies in large quantities from the manufacturers, food processors, publishers, etc. It has a large packing house in Philadelphia where the food packages and self-aid kits are prepared. The organization also deals directly with the shipping lines which transport its materials.

CARE has special agents in each port where the ships dock. These agents arrange the transportation over land to the various destinations of the packages. Through the cooperation of the countries involved, CARE packages are admitted duty-free. The agents also oversee the warehouses where the materials are stored until delivery, and spot-check occasionally to be sure everything is being handled properly.

CARE has always stressed the importance of person-to-person sharing. It feels that each package that goes out from America carries along with it a message of friendship from the donor. That is why personal contributions of any amount are welcomed. Persons contributing to CARE may specify to which of the countries where CARE operates they wish their contribution to go and the type of supply they wish to send. Or, if they prefer, they may leave the choice to CARE. Either way, CARE acknowledges the contribution and reports where and how the money was spent.

What goes in each CARE package depends on the country that is receiving the shipment. Diets of people differ, depending on where they live, and the type of food varies accordingly. Also the number of food packages sent to a particular country depends to a large extent on whether the country recently has been the victim of a natural disaster. For example, a crop failure in Iran means that in that year food will be scarcer than usual. Poland has had a series of serious floods and has needed food badly. The rice crops in South Vietnam have been destroyed by Communist guerilla raids and one time a herd of wild elephants trampled down the rice paddies. In some countries food prices are so high that poor people cannot afford to buy enough to keep from being hungry. During the winter months the number of food package deliveries exceeds that of the summer months. In the case of a sudden disaster such as a flood or earthquake food packages are rushed immediately to the victims.

Sometimes an organization that is a member of CARE assumes a long-time project. The General Federation of Women's Clubs (GFWC) is one of these agencies. Working through CARE, it lent its aid to a town in Colombia, South America. This town depended for a large part of its economy on the banana industry, but a dreaded disease attacked the banana trees and destroyed the entire crop. For many people this meant their incomes ceased and times were difficult. There were no public schools and most of the people could no longer afford to send their children to the private and parochial schools. Juvenile delinquency was on the increase as the children roamed the streets with nothing to do.

Finally a few of the citizens got together and decided something must be done about conditions that were getting out of hand so rapidly. They formed a Society for the Protection of Children and, as their first step, rented a building that could be used as a school. Then they secured the services of a public-spirited teacher who agreed to work for practically nothing. CARE and the GFWC heard about the project and offered to help. Blackboards and other classroom supplies were furnished. As the school flourished there was demand for others to open too. Besides books and playground equipment CARE and GFWC now began to include kits for plumbers, electricians and carpenters. With these do-it-yourself aids the citizens got busy and soon another school was on its way to completion. But this was not all. People who heretofore had been content to live in huts began to take more pride in their homes and soon their dwellings could boast of doors and windows! Adults asked for night school classes, and industrial and agricultural methods were studied along with health and hygiene. A town whose citizens had once despaired of life itself was beginning to live again.

CARE has extended its activities in other fields too. Near Rome, Italy, there is a Children's Spastic Center. CARE has given wheel chairs, books, play equipment, a plastic swimming pool and even a bus for transporting the children from their homes to the school.

In Athens, Greece, CARE furnishes tools to a rehabilitation center so that disabled persons can be taught a trade and thus become self-supporting.

In Turkey, CARE donated a mobile health unit which travels throughout the country. Persons who visit it not only get medical attention but are also instructed in good hygiene.

In South Korea, CARE has been providing boats for fishermen so that they can be independent and take care of their families. Livestock has been sent to persons living inland to help restock their farms. Sewing machines have been given to war widows who needed means to earn a livelihood. Surplus food, blankets, clothing and books for the schools have been brought in.

Since 1945, when CARE was first founded, there have been many new developments in the world. New nations have been born and along with them new problems. And always there are the old problems of hunger and frustration which lead to unrest among the people. But always, too, there is the hope that someday life is going to be better.

With all these world changes that have been occurring CARE has had to change too. It has had to expand at a rapid rate but it has tried to keep its spirit of personal friendship the same. One of its most recent changes was announced early in 1962. This was its merger with MEDICO.

MEDICO

When one thinks of MEDICO, one instinctively thinks of Dr. Tom Dooley and the enthusiasm with which he worked for this organization so dear to his heart. Up until his fatal illness he barnstormed around the country, telling people what it was doing and raising funds for it by the sheer force of his personality.

MEDICO, which means Medical International Cooperation Organization, was the brainchild of Dr. Tom Dooley and Dr. Peter C. Commanduras, a well-known physician in Washington and an Associate Professor of Clinical Medicine at Georgetown University. The two doctors had been corresponding for some time while Dr. Dooley was running his hospitals in Laos, but had never met. In the fall of 1957,

Dr. Dooley returned to the United States and he and Dr. Commanduras arranged a meeting.

Even in their first conversation together they found they shared many ideas as to how medical aid could be carried on throughout the world. Dr. Commanduras had long believed that this should be done by private doctors without any government aid. He had approached several foreign aid officers with this idea but somehow, perhaps because his plan sounded too simple, he had failed to get it across. He was delighted when Dr. Dooley told him he was in complete agreement and that aid could be given simply with comparatively little expense.

Dr. Dooley had been operating his hospitals in Laos under the sponsorship of the International Rescue Committee. He planned to go before the Committee to give a report of his work in Laos and to request financial help to continue. Dr. Dooley and Dr. Commanduras worked out together a plan for future expansion which Dr. Dooley presented to the Committee. This covered a sixteen-month period and entailed sending six teams of medical workers into the field.

When Dr. Dooley first presented this plan to the Committee the members argued it couldn't be done. There was nothing in the Constitution of the International Rescue Committee to permit it. But Dr. Dooley finally won them over and they decided to change their constitution in order to give him the help he requested. Thus MEDICO, the Medical International Cooperation Organization, was born. Dr. Commanduras and Dr. Dooley did not intend that MEDICO should replace any existing agency that was already working in the field of health such as WHO, the United Nations World Health Organization. Rather it was to function on a person-to-person basis. They believed that friendships could be made by working with persons on their own level in a simple way.

When MEDICO became a reality, Dr. Commanduras gave up his practice of medicine to devote his entire time to the management of the new organization. Dr. Dooley called him "The Secretary-General of MEDICO." After a cross-country tour of lectures to raise money for MEDICO, Dooley returned to Laos to oversee the establishing of additional MEDICO hospitals.

By 1959, MEDICO had reached the place where it was felt it should leave the International Rescue Committee and set itself up as a separate organization. Just at that time Dr. Dooley was forced to come home for a cancer operation. But he didn't let it interfere with his enthusiasm for MEDICO and after his release from the hospital he went on another lecture tour to raise funds for it.

As time went on MEDICO continued to expand. And as it expanded it had to change its concept from the one the doctors had envisioned in the beginning. In some places it could still keep the village-type hospital. But it had to adapt itself to conditions, and in more advanced countries something better than a primitive hospital had to be established.

By the middle of 1960 the field personnel of MEDICO included twelve physicians and surgeons, and more than thirty nurses and corpsmen were on duty in various hospitals. And all the time more and more applications were being received and screened by Dr. Commanduras in New York.

Toward the end of 1960 Dr. Tom Dooley had a recurrence of cancer and died in January, 1961, shortly after his return to the United States. Before his death, however, he had seen the nation respond to his pleas for MEDICO far beyond anything he had imagined.

Since that time MEDICO has continued to grow. Its resources, its ambitions and the scope of its work have increased constantly. By 1962, it had or was in the process of organizing seventeen hospitals in remote jungle or mountain areas. Each one has been established because the host government requested it.

Besides setting up its own hospitals MEDICO also provides some of the equipment and drugs for those hospitals which were in existence before it was formed. Drug companies have responded generously to its pleas for help and during a period of two years contributed drugs and medical supplies worth more than three million dollars.

Because of the amount of business organization that is needed as its growth continues, MEDICO has merged with CARE, which has had more than fifteen years of experience in the field of distributing food and self-help assistance. MEDICO is thus left free to concentrate on healing the sick rather than expending its time in dealing with the mechanics of securing supplies and transporting them where they are needed.

Americans can indeed be proud of these two organizations which are dedicated to people who are sick, hungry or in need of someone to lend a helping hand—CARE and MEDICO.

CARING FOR THE SICK

*They helped every one his neighbor: and every
one said to his brother, Be of good courage.*

—Isaiah 41:6

It is hard for us, living in the United States where medical service is readily available, to realize that there are parts of the world where it is unknown. Millions of people living in primitive areas have suffered unaided from many diseases. These have been brought on for the most part through ignorance of good health rules, lack of sanitation and malnutrition. Superstitious natives, with their age-old belief in magic, consulted witch doctors for cures only trained doctors and surgeons could have effected.

There have been many devoted missionaries throughout the years who have spent their lives helping unfortunate people. In 1870, when Father Damien went to Molokai to treat the lepers, they were considered unclean and were deserted by mankind. Father Damien and other self-sacrificing persons in different parts of the world paved the way for the work which was to follow in the medical field.

Three doctors, whose names are world-famous, dedicated their lives to establishing hospitals in remote places: Dr. Albert Schweitzer in Africa, Dr. Gordon Seagrave in Burma and Dr. Tom Dooley in Laos.

One of the most recent endeavors to take medical aid to underdeveloped countries is the Ship of Hope. This, a project of the American people, is a true example of person-to-person brotherhood.

Father Damien

What were Father Damien's thoughts as he stood on the beach at Molokai that day in 1870, knowing that this lonely, deserted spot was to be his home—that these poor, diseased creatures gathered to greet him were to be his parishioners? Everywhere he looked there was desolation. The only homes he could see were a few tottering grass huts that were falling apart; the land itself was barren of crops and almost devoid of trees; the scanty water supply was only that which was carried from afar in pails. And, what was worse, the only people there were ravaged by leprosy, their disease apparent in their scarred and ugly faces and their poor crippled hands and limping feet. The fate that had brought him seemed to be saying, "Here you are on the Great Gray Island. It is yours. Do with it whatever you can."

Molokai was called the Great Gray Island because, of all the beautiful Hawaiian group, it was the least attractive island, with great gray walls of rock standing high above the sea like silent sentinels: prison walls for those who had been exiled there. It was the involuntary home of the lepers, that cheerless army whose future held no hope of cure and whose lives had to be forever spent in that awful place.

And yet the priest, Father Damien, had begged his superiors to let him come here. What manner of man was this who, when all other men shunned the island and hated its very name, had cast his lot with lepers, the most miserable of all creatures upon the face of the earth?

He was born Joseph de Veuster on January 3, 1840, on a farm in Tremeloo in Belgium, the seventh child of Francois and Catherine de Veuster. His parents were simple, hard-working farm folk whose ambition was to give their children a good education. Joseph's older brother Auguste and his sister Pauline were chosen by their parents for the religious life of the Church, while Joseph, his father decided, was to become the businessman of the family. But very early in his life the boy Joseph revealed a spiritual quality in his nature. One morning when he was only four years old, after having been missing from his home and searched for for hours, he was found in the village chapel on his knees before the altar.

Joseph loved his father's farm and performed dutifully all the chores he was given to do. The neighbors called him the Little Shepherd because his fondest duty was to herd his father's sheep along the banks of the Laak River. There he could sit alone and meditate and reflect, as his heroes the saints and martyrs had done. He knew all about them from having listened with the other children as his mother read aloud to them from a great thick book called *The Lives of the Holy Martyrs and Hermits*. Joseph wished he could grow up to be a religious man like those in the book. His mother knew about his secret longings, for when she made up his bed one morning she found he had been sleeping on a board like the hermits! And more than once in the night she had gone into the boys' room to find little Joseph sleeping on the floor.

When he started to school the other children nicknamed him Silent Joseph. In spite of this, he was admired by the others for his strength and athletic ability. No boy in his class could whip him.

Though Joseph, as he grew out of his childhood, gave up the game of playing hermit, he never forgot his ambition to enter the religious life. He envied his brother Auguste when he became a candidate for the priesthood with the Picpus Fathers and changed his name to Pamphile. Likewise he envied his sister Pauline when she entered a convent to become a nun. When he was eighteen he was a student in a college at Braine-le-Comte, learning to become a businessman, but his heart was not in it. His sole ambition was to enter the Church. And finally, after much persuading, he gained his father's permission to do so. On his nineteenth birthday, his father took him to the Picpus Fathers where his brother was, and he was immediately accepted. At last Joseph was launched on the life he had longed for since he was a little boy.

Joseph's education had not followed the same lines as his brother's, however, and at first he was not qualified to become a candidate for the priesthood. So he became a lay brother. Undaunted, he began secretly to learn Latin from his brother Pamphile. It was not long before his qualifications were apparent to his superiors. Anyone whose desire to be a priest was so great could not easily be refused. He became a candidate for the priesthood. From now on his name was Damien. In 1860, Damien took the threefold vow of "poverty, chastity and obedience."

Before he had ever been ordained, however, something happened to Damien that was destined to take him far across the sea, eventually to Molokai the Gray, where he was to spend the remainder of his life. It happened in this way.

The Picpus Fathers, of whom Damien and Pamphile were a part, maintained missions in the Sandwich Islands, as the Hawaiian group was then known. When Father Pamphile received his orders to serve there he was overjoyed that this was to be his mission. But an epidemic of typhus was rampant just at this time and, unfortunately, Father Pamphile fell dangerously ill with the disease.

Damien visited his brother daily. When Father Pamphile was not too ill to talk to Damien, all he could do was lament the fact that he couldn't go.

"I have been thinking," Damien said to him one day. "I could go in your place."

"But you aren't even ordained," Father Pamphile answered. "They would never let you go."

But Damien was not one to give up easily. Instead of asking permission of his immediate superiors, he wrote directly to the Father General himself. The reply surprised even the optimistic Damien; it was yes! Father Pamphile's place was to be taken by Damien, and soon he would be setting off on the long journey.

But first he must go home and say good-bye to his family. He paid a short visit to them in Tremeloo; then he left. But the next morning at the lovely shrine of Our Blessed Mother at Montaigu, he met his mother in the cold dawn of early Mass, and there they said their good-byes. It was the last time he was ever to see her.

With one priest, five lay brothers, and several Sisters of the Sacred Heart, he boarded a train from Paris to Bremerhaven. There the Hawaiian merchant ship *H. M. Wood* was ready to take them on their journey. The voyage took five months. On March 19, 1864, Damien arrived in Hawaii. There he was ordained a priest and, on the happiest day of his life, served his first Mass in the Cathedral of Our Lady of Peace in Honolulu.

On the Island of Hawaii, Father Damien was assigned to the parish of Puna, where he served for nine years. With the help of the natives there he built churches, doing much of the work with his own hands. He was so strong that he could carry boards so heavy it took three or four men to lift them into position.

One of Father Damien's helpers at Puna was a young native boy, a fine, strong lad whose life was suddenly made tragic when the dreaded disease of leprosy struck him down. He disappeared and Father Damien believed the boy must have been taken to Molokai.

Leprosy had been brought to the Islands by immigrants from Asia many years before, but now it was spreading so rapidly that the Hawaiian government felt that drastic steps must be taken to protect the healthy. Finally in 1865 the government passed an act which declared that lepers must report for inspection. From there they were to be banished to the Island of Molokai. There were, in those days, no cures. This meant total exile for life.

Unfortunately for the people who were sent there, the Hawaiian government had set aside no money for dwelling places and very little for food, clothing and supplies. Occasionally a ship would land at the island and a few very inadequate supplies would be dropped off for the destitute. This was the almost hopeless situation among some eight hundred lepers on the island when Father Damien landed there in 1870. And why had he come?

As usual with the young priest, it was his great desire to serve humanity. One of a congregation of missionaries, he had listened one memorable day to a talk by the Bishop of Honolulu. In his talk the Bishop described the terrible conditions on Molokai. He spoke of the requests the lepers had made from time to time to have a priest sent out to them. "Unfortunately, there seems to be nothing we can do for these poor creatures," the Bishop said, and explained that he could not find it in his heart to condemn any priest in his diocese to such a life. It was then that Father Damien begged his Bishop to be allowed to go. The Bishop reminded Damien of what such a life would mean. "You will, of course, be an exile, never able again to associate with other men who are free of the disease."

Father Damien assured the Bishop that he understood all this. In his eagerness to go, he was overjoyed to learn that a leper ship with fifty victims aboard was now in the harbor and would leave almost at once. The eager young priest, accompanied by the Bishop who would see him to his destination, boarded the ship. There was no time for him to get his few personal belongings from Puna. He went as he was, a tall, erect figure in a black cassock and plain black hat. He was thirty-three years old. His real mission had begun.

After the Bishop and the ship in which they had arrived had departed, Father Damien's first act was to fashion an improvised broom from branches and sweep out the dirty little hut that had served as a chapel for the occasional visiting missionaries who had stopped at the island to say Mass. He spent that first night lying on the gnarled roots of a huge pandanus tree because there was no shelter for him. And this was the priest's bed for weeks, for he was too busy building new shelters for the very ill to take the time to build one for himself. In keeping with the hopelessness of the disease, he found the lepers completely indifferent to the state of conditions on the island. They had done nothing to try to improve their unsanitary, actually filthy, way of living, accepting it as a part of their hopeless status in life. In fact, there were many whose attitude toward the new arrival and his desire to help them was one of suspicion and open hostility. But Father Damien knew there were some who could be roused from their lethargy. Daily he found some soul who still had a spark of interest and was willing to follow his suggestions. The people grew hopeful at the sight of the healthy young man in his black robes with his rosary in one hand and his hammer in the other. One by one they came to him and offered to help. Little by little, clean new huts appeared. As soon as the Father could get word back to Hawaii, he sent for and received new lumber. With the help of some who had been carpenters by trade, he made possible the cheerful signs of improvement no one had dreamed would ever take place.

One of the greatest contributions he made was a new water system. Until his arrival, all water had to be carried from a place far up in the hills. Father Damien requested and received pipes from the government and these brought fresh water within reach of the people. At last there was plenty of water to keep them and their clothing clean. Another thing that had been a great worry to the priest was the drunkenness that had existed among many of the lepers. In their dejection, they had turned to making an alcoholic beverage they called *ki*. The constant drinking of *ki* had caused much trouble among the people until Damien, who could be stern when sternness was demanded, gradually got them to give up the vessels in which they had made their drink. The drunkenness stopped.

Among the lepers he recognized many whom he had known in his ministry at Puna, and among these was the young lad who had helped him there. Although the disease so far had done little damage to him physically, mentally he was dejected and would not mingle with the others. He showed no interest in living. Like many of the others, he felt that life, for him, was over. Rousing his interest became a daily task for the priest and, finally, the lad left his hut and joined Father Damien at his work. Again they became fast friends.

It was nothing short of miraculous, the changes the priest was able to make in the weeks and months that followed on the Great Gray Isle! New, clean huts appeared everywhere, as well as a hospital where the very ill patients could be laid on clean beds and treated so that, even if they could not be cured, they could die in peace. This was made possible by medical supplies sent from the Hawaiian government and the presence of a real doctor, a leper, who assisted Father Damien in ministering to the sick.

As the years went on, the improvements continued. Father Damien's work became well known in other parts of the world, and more and more supplies, clothing and medicines were sent to the lepers. And a dream of Damien's came true when orphanages were built, one for the boys and one for the girls. There were two churches, one serving each of the two settlements on the island, and at each of these there were choirs trained by Father Damien, who had finally interested the lepers in music and singing.

When Father Damien had been on the island eight years, the Bishop of Honolulu visited Molokai and decorated the priest with the Cross of Knight Commander of the King. But probably the most exciting time for the residents of Molokai was the day the Queen of Hawaii, Liliuokalani, came to visit the lepers. Eight hundred people were there to greet her as she and those who accompanied her were escorted from ship to shore in flower-bedecked boats. On shore, she was led to a tented platform from which she could watch the ceremonies. The girls' chorus sang for her, a beautiful Hawaiian song that caused her to weep. She spent the day on the island and was taken on a grand tour to see all the improvements on Molokai. When it came time for her to leave, she thanked Father Damien for all he had done for her poor exiles. "I shall never forget," she told him.

And she did not forget. She sent many gifts to the lepers.

One of the chief characteristics of Father Damien in all the years of his life as a priest, both at Puna and at Molokai, had been his exceeding good health. In any sort of manual work he excelled because of his great physical strength. His healthy body and his glowing, cheerful face must have been a source of inspiration to the hundreds of patients with whom he worked. And yet perhaps there were some who felt he could not fully understand them because of this same physical perfection which set him apart.

One day when preaching to them, the Father's change of words struck strangely on their ears. Instead of saying, "You lepers," he said, "We lepers . . ." Before long the entire island knew the truth. Father Damien was now one of them; he was a leper.

It had not happened suddenly. Little signals had warned him. And then one night when he placed his tired feet in scalding hot water to bathe them, the truth suddenly became apparent. He could not feel the hot water though it was almost boiling and caused his feet to turn red. The next day the doctor confirmed his suspicions. The disease had finally struck him.

This was in 1884, more than fourteen years after his work had begun on the island. Father Damien was to live five years longer. He was to see the fruits of his labor come to harvest.

In the last years of his life the priest became less and less active and eventually an invalid from the debilitating disease that now racked his body. But his spirit was never daunted, and he felt and expressed his gratitude to God for having sent him so many helpers. Two priests, two lay brothers and three Sisters of Charity, along with a full-time resident doctor, now comprised his staff. What made Father Damien even happier was the way the lepers were helping themselves. The two settlements were flourishing, with communication and visiting between them. The people lived cleanly in their new houses. They took part in the work of raising crops and vegetables. They wove mats and performed other handicraft miracles with their ofttimes crippled fingers. They took active interest in the Church and other affairs of the community. The hospital and the schools for the children flourished. Damien, with his never-failing faith in the lepers, had worked a miracle.

Among those whom Damien rejoiced to have as his assistants was an American by the name of Ira Dutton. He had come to the island in July, 1886, and offered his services to Father Damien with the simple words, "I have come to help you." In an old newspaper he had read of Father Damien's work on Molokai and had promptly come to the decision to spend the remainder of his life there, hoping that he could be of use. "Brother Joseph's" wish came true, for it was he, on the death of Father Damien, who became head of the mission.

After many long weeks of suffering, Father Damien on April 15, 1889, breathed his last. Among the last words he spoke were words of gratitude. "How good God is! The work of the lepers is assured and so I am no longer necessary and will go up yonder."

The work on Molokai begun by him so many years before was not over. It would go on—for thus good deeds outlive the mortal life of those who perform them. This was true of Father Damien, who had given the last full measure of his devotion.

Dr. Albert Schweitzer

The operation is finished, and in the hardly lighted dormitory I watch for the sick man's awaking. Scarcely has he recovered consciousness when he stares about him and ejaculates again and again: 'I've no more pain! I've no more pain!' . . . His hand feels for mine and will not let it go. Then I begin to tell him and the others who are in the room that it is the Lord Jesus who has told the doctor and his wife to come to the Ogowé, and that white people in Europe give them the money to live here and cure the sick Negroes. Then I have to answer questions as to who these white people are, where they live, and how they know that the natives suffer so much from sickness. The African sun is shining

*through the coffee bushes into the dark shed, but we black and
white sit side by side and feel that we know by experience the
meaning of the words: 'And all ye are brethren' (Matt. xxiii:8).*

—ALBERT SCHWEITZER
FROM *On the Edge of the Primeval Forest*

Millions of words have been written about Dr. Albert Schweitzer.
By many people in many lands he is considered the greatest man of
our age. When his life and accomplishments are reviewed, it is natural
to ask the question that often occurs to us when we think of a man of
fame: what is it that makes this man great?

Albert Schweitzer is a man of many talents, all of them developed
to the point of success. Musician, organ-builder, teacher, writer, doctor, theologian and philosopher; as each he became world famous.
As a musician he was sensitive to the beauty of the world's great music
and able to translate it; as an organ-builder he was contented only with
perfection; as teacher and writer he was able to express his thoughts
verbally and with the pen; as doctor he was conscious of the suffering
in the world; and as theologian and philosopher he sought the deeper
meanings of life. Above all, throughout his life Albert Schweitzer
was influenced by his faith in God and his kinship with his fellow man.

Albert Schweitzer's father and grandfather were ministers, his
paternal grandfather a teacher and musician. The son of Louis and
Adele Schweitzer, Albert was born in Kaysersberg, Upper Alsace,
on January 14, 1875. Almost immediately the family moved to Gunsbach, where his father was the Protestant pastor of the only church in
the town. The church was unusual in that it served not only the Protestant but also the Catholic congregation. As a child Albert enjoyed
the Sunday sermons preached by his Protestant father and the rituals
of the Catholic Mass. Most of all, the small boy thrilled to the music
of the church organ. When he was only eight years old and his legs
were almost too short to reach the pedals, he began to play the organ.
A year later he played for the service when the organist failed to show
up.

When Albert was nine, he left the village school and went to live
in the house of his great-uncle in Mulhausen where he attended the
gymnasium, or high school. There he studied organ under Eugene

Munch, to whom he attributed his lifelong appreciation of Bach's music. After he had graduated from this school he became an organ pupil of the famous Parisian musician Charles Louis Widor. When he entered the University of Strasbourg, he continued to study with Widor.

At the University he studied theology and philosophy in preparation for a ministerial career. Even when he entered upon the required year of military training in the spring of 1894, he was able, through arrangement with his superior officer, to attend lectures at the University. The ambitious young Albert was probably the only soldier who went off on maneuvers with a Greek Testament in his haversack. He had chosen the Synoptic Gospels as his subject for the examination he would have to pass in order to win a scholarship.

In the fall of 1897, he presented himself as candidate for the theological examination. The subject of his thesis was the Last Supper. After he had passed his first theological examination he moved to Paris and continued his studies at the famous Sorbonne University. In July, 1899, he received the degree of Doctor of Philosophy.

In December of that year Albert began his career as a theologian by being assigned to the St. Nicholas Church in Strasbourg. One of his duties was to work with children. His teaching experience began there in the confirmation classes. In later years he was thanked by some of those who took his classes for having instilled in them at that early age the basic truths taught by Jesus.

One of the things that made this a fulfilled and contented period in his life was that it gave him time to devote to his music. In all the previous years of his education he had never neglected it, for music was one of his greatest loves. From the time he had first gone to Paris he had studied organ under Widor, and the piano under another teacher. From a fine teacher who had studied under Franz Liszt, he also studied touch playing, a system involving the manner in which the keys are pressed down and released. So filled were his student days that sometimes when he went to Widor for his lesson in the morning he had not been to bed the night before at all.

And now as curate at St. Nicholas he continued with his music, his scientific work and his writing. He was working on his study of the Last Supper, a book on the life of Jesus and another on Johann Sebastian Bach. The days were crowded. But always, in spite of the many things he had to think about, there was in the back of his mind a decision he was trying to make. What, ultimately, would he do with his life? This was not a new thought. Indeed, for several years he had been trying to make this decision. It had all begun on a bright summer morning while he was at home in Gunsbach. The birds had wakened him and for a while he had lain in his bed thinking of all his good fortune, asking himself what he could do in return for the natural gifts and circumstances of his happy life. Thereupon he made a vow, pledging to himself that beginning on his thirtieth birthday he would seriously begin to serve mankind.

When he was appointed principal of the Theological Seminary of Strasbourg in 1903, Schweitzer found time to do volunteer work with neglected children. For a time he thought that this might become his channel of service. Another time he became interested in helping tramps and ex-convicts. There were other thoughts on how best to serve humanity. And then, one day in the fall of 1904, he suddenly found the answer to his question. Someone had laid on his desk a magazine that was put out monthly by the Paris Missionary Society. As he was about to lay it aside, he glanced at the contents and noticed that it contained an article entitled, "The Needs of the Congo Mission." He sat down and read the piece describing the need for workers in the Gaboon province of the Congo. It ended with the statement: "Men and women who can reply simply to the Master's call, 'Lord, I am coming,' those are the people whom the church needs." Albert Schweitzer knew that this was his call to service.

After his decision had been reached, Albert Schweitzer quietly began to make his plans. But when his intention became known to his relatives and friends he was surprised to find himself facing stiff opposition. They tried to dissuade him, using the argument that he would certainly be wasting his talents. How could the savages of Africa possibly appreciate a man with his education and abilities? Dr. Schweitzer in his autobiography later said how grateful he was to those friends who tried to understand his motives. One of these was Helene Bresslau, the daughter of the Strasbourg historian. In her he found he had a sympathetic listener when he spoke of his plans. And now those plans included a number of years of hard study ahead, for Albert had decided to become a physician.

This was not an easy decision to make. With all the years of study behind him, the scientific field of medicine would mean another start in an entirely new world. He dreaded the years of preparation, but he knew enough about conditions in the part of Africa where he was going to realize that the greatest help he could give would be as a doctor. And so, at the age of thirty in 1905, he went to attend his first lecture in anatomy at the University of Strasbourg.

Thus began the busiest seven years of his life. While studying medicine he also continued to lecture on theology, to preach on Sunday, and to maintain his often grueling work as organist at the concerts and recitals of the Paris Bach Society. He also, somehow, found time to write. In 1906 his book *The Quest of the Historical Jesus* was published. Many consider it Schweitzer's masterpiece.

In October of 1911 he took the State Medical Examination. This was followed by a year's volunteer work in hospitals. Finally, in the spring of 1912, he gave up his work at the University and his preaching at St. Nicholas. These two resignations made him acutely aware of the sacrifice he was making, for he believed that his well-loved careers of preaching and lecturing were over. In June he and Helene Bresslau were married and went to Gunsbach to spend the last few months in the parsonage with his parents.

His time of preparation was over. He had spent months raising money for his African trip and then purchasing, listing and packing the supplies they were to take with them. Money for these things had been given generously by his congregation at St. Nicholas and the faculty members of the University. Another source had been a benefit concert given by the Paris Bach Society. Thus, the friends who at first had tried to prevent him from going to Africa now supported him in the enterprise. When the future of his hospital was fairly well ensured, he offered his services to the Paris Missionary Society, to serve at his own expense in mission work on the River Ogowé. He would serve out of the central mission settlement at Lambaréné. This mission had been started in 1876 by an American missionary but had been taken over by the Paris Missionary Society in 1892. His offer was accepted.

In February, 1913, the seventy packing cases filled with supplies began their journey toward their destination. On March twenty-sixth the Schweitzers left Bordeaux for Lambaréné. In spite of the regrets at leaving his home, his parents and friends and the life that had been so rich in accomplishments, he was looking forward to a life of service. He was strong, healthy, eager and determined. His wife, who had taken nurse's training and was also eager to serve, was his helpmate. They would enter upon the new life together.

After several weeks, the Schweitzers disembarked from their ship at Libreville. Then from Cape Lopez they took a steamer up the yellowish waters of the broad Ogowé River. Two days in oppressive heat between tropical trees and muddy banks on which crocodiles were sleeping, and at last the little boat reached the island on which the tiny town of Lambaréné was situated. They finished the last lap of their fantastic journey in long, narrow, native canoes. As the canoes pulled up on the bank, the Schweitzers were greeted enthusiastically by the white missionaries and numerous black natives.

The hearty welcome was somewhat dampened for the doctor and his wife when they discovered that the corrugated iron buildings that had been planned for their hospital had not been built because of lack of labor; but to Dr. Schweitzer this was no reason for not beginning his work at once. The cases were unpacked, and even before the boxes were emptied, he began seeing patients in "an old fowl house" near their living quarters.

It was not long before the doctor could see the advantage of the location of Lambaréné. Situated as it was on the long Ogowé River, it was available to patients from upstream or downstream, and by canoe they came distances as great as two hundred miles. They came by the hundreds! Before long, Dr. Schweitzer was treating cases of malaria, sleeping sickness, leprosy, dysentery, pneumonia, heart disease, ulcers, tumors and hernia. Every day he felt more rewarded that he had come to Lambaréné as a doctor.

Madame Schweitzer was everywhere at once, nursing the sick, administering anaesthesia for the operations, taking care of the instruments and applying bandages to wounds. Besides this she kept house under difficulties that only a jungle in equatorial Africa could present to a housewife.

By autumn, Dr. Schweitzer moved into his new building made of corrugated iron, twenty-six feet by thirteen, with a roof of palm leaves. It contained an operating room, a small consulting room and a tiny dispensary. Gradually, small huts of bamboo were built to house the patients. Before long there were forty "in" patients—

those who needed hospital care. Also to be accommodated were the families who came with the patients to take care of them. As for payment, a few of the natives paid the doctor in money, but for the most part he was paid in bananas, poultry and eggs. Labor was another form of payment offered by some industrious ones. The mission soon took on the characteristics of a native village, with each family a unit, taking care of their sick member, doing their cooking in their crude ways with the utensils they had brought from home. From the start, Dr. Schweitzer gave these people the right to live at the settlement in their accustomed way, for he soon discovered that only under such conditions were patients content to remain until the required treatment was finished.

And so the busy months passed. Dr. Schweitzer had been asked by the Mission to help with the preaching, and this gave him much pleasure. As he preached, his words were translated sentence by sentence by his assistant, Joseph, a native who spoke French. As for his "spare time," it was used in working on his projected three-volume work on Bach's organ music which he was preparing for American publication. And still he found time to play the beloved piano which had been presented to him by the Paris Bach Society and was especially built to withstand the tropical climate.

Then in August of 1914 the hospital work suddenly came to a standstill. War had been declared on France by Germany. Because the Schweitzers were German citizens in French territory, they were declared prisoners of war. Guards were placed over them to see that they had no communication with outsiders. Undaunted, Dr. Schweitzer began work on his book, *The Philosophy of Civilization*. Within a few months he was again permitted to work in his hospital.

It was in September of 1915 that a great revelation of the basic meaning of his existence came to Dr. Schweitzer. It happened as he was going by steamer up the river to visit the wife of a sick missionary. As usual, he had pencil and pad with him, and as the boat made its tortuous way up the river, he sat writing and meditating. On the third day, just at sunset, the boat passed through a herd of hippopotamuses. Suddenly Dr. Schweitzer's thoughts were crowded out by three words that imprinted themselves on his mind. The words were, "reverence for life." In his autobiography, *Out of My Life and Thought*, he tells of this incident and what it meant to him. He explains that a man can be moral only when all life is sacred to him— not only that of his fellow men but also of plants and animals. Furthermore, that man's moral responsibility lies in devoting himself to those who need help. Albert Schweitzer not only believed in this philosophy with all his heart but practiced it from day to day.

In September of 1917, the Schweitzers were ordered back to Europe. They were taken to a large prisoner-of-war camp in the Pyrenees Mountains called Garaison. There, as the only doctor, he was finally permitted to treat the sick prisoners. Later he and Madame Schweitzer were transferred to another prison camp, and then to their great joy they were sent home to Alsace! They had both suffered from the close confinement, and after returning to Strasbourg Dr. Schweitzer underwent surgery. It was not long after his recuperation that he began to work in the municipal hospital at Strasbourg and also had his old job back as curate of St. Nicholas Church. Then, in November, 1918, the Armistice came. The war was over.

But more preparations would be necessary before the doctor could go back to Lambaréné. First of all, there were debts contracted in Lambaréné that had to be paid. To help this situation, he followed the advice of his Archbishop and wrote about his African experiences. *On the Edge of the Primeval Forest* not only helped to clear his debts but made him well known, for it was translated into many languages. As a further means of raising money, he spent several years giving concerts and lectures in Sweden, Switzerland, England and Denmark. Now he was ready to go back to Lambaréné.

In many ways this second trip to Africa would be harder than the first. His enthusiastic reception as a world-renowned organist and his great success as a lecturer made him fully aware of the fact that he was turning his back on almost unlimited success in Europe. Personal ties also bound him to his place in civilization, for this time Madame Schweitzer would have to remain at home to care for their small daughter Rhena. The Schweitzers felt that they could not subject the small child to the heat and diseases of the tropics. But Albert Schweitzer knew in his heart where his service was most needed. On February 21, 1924, he started back to Lambaréné.

On the ship he ran into trouble with the customs officer over his strange cargo of four potato sacks full of letters that he had received from his admirers and to which he intended to reply while on shipboard. Because there was a strict law about taking money out of France at that time, the officer looked with suspicion upon the sacks of correspondence, but after spending an hour and a half looking through the piles of letters, he gave up. He was ready to concede that these were what Dr. Schweitzer had claimed, letters written to one person!

On Easter Eve, Dr. Schweitzer and the medical student who accompanied him arrived in Lambaréné. The doctor was filled with dismay at what he saw. With the exception of his bungalow and one corrugated iron building (that without a roof) the hospital had disintegrated—rotted away!

For several months he played the role of physician by morning and carpenter by afternoon. Progress was slow because he had scarcely any help. It took two years before the buildings were all again erected. By this time he had received help from Europe in the form of two doctors and two nurses.

But again there was a mountain of work to be done, for circumstances forced the removal of the hospital to a site two miles farther up the river. Here there was room to expand the hospital to the greater size it now required for the ever-increasing number of patients. For this immense project Dr. Schweitzer found it necessary to turn most of the medical work over to the other doctors, because the natives refused to take orders from anyone but "the old doctor." First the site was cleared, with agonizing slowness, of its wild vegetation. Then the construction of the corrugated iron buildings began. Every night the doctor-builder was so exhausted that any thought of continuing with his writing was impossible.

In January, 1927, when the new hospital was opened, a brand new motor boat, the gift of the women of Sweden, helped to ease the task of transferring the patients on the two-mile trip up the river. Up to that time the only mode of transportation on the river had been canoes. The joy of the patients at being in clean beds in their new hospital wards, and the satisfaction of the staff in working with their improved facilities, spread an aura of sunshine over the place. Work continued throughout that spring and summer until the hospital could accommodate two hundred patients and provide shelters for their families. To Dr. Schweitzer's great satisfaction, the hospital now contained an entire building for mental patients, as well as the isolation ward he had so sorely needed ever since his first patients, many of them with communicable diseases, came to Lambaréné. At last, with the hospital all moved and settled in its new quarters, Dr. Schweitzer felt that he could leave to visit his wife and daughter. In July he went back to Alsace after having been away for three and a half years.

There followed two years of lecturing and giving concerts to raise money for Lambaréné, during which time he also prepared a new book for publication. By this time, Dr. Schweitzer and his hospital were so well known that raising funds to carry on the work was an easier task. Gifts poured in from all over Europe, not only from organizations and wealthy individuals, but from poor people who wanted to help. The doctor was deeply touched by the generosity of so many souls.

It was during this stay in Europe that Albert Schweitzer's father died. The old parsonage at Gunsbach was no longer his home. Before the doctor left again for Lambaréné, he was able to build a modest home in Gunsbach to which he was to return for visits off and on for many years. Schweitzer called it "the house that Goethe built" because he had received the money to build it in 1928 when he won the Goethe Prize for his scholarly address on that great German poet.

When he returned again to Lambaréné, he was accompanied by his wife, a new doctor and a laboratory technician. Rhena was left in Europe to receive her education.

The next ten years were busy ones for Albert Schweitzer, with his time divided between being doctor, preacher and writer at Lambaréné, and musician, lecturer and writer in the countries of Europe. People marveled at his energy. On a tour of England in 1932 he kept to a sixteen-hour day. Many times before an organ recital he practiced eight hours at a stretch. While in England he received four honorary degrees. Invitations came from all the important universities of Europe to lecture on philosophy. Through the translation of his books into many languages, his fame had spread throughout the world.

The twenty-fifth anniversary of the founding of the hospital at Lambaréné took place in 1938, and to commemorate it the European population of the Ogowé region presented him with ninety thousand francs. The money was intended for the purchase of an

X-ray machine, but the doctor obtained permission instead to buy a large amount of badly needed drug supplies. With political conditions as they were in Europe, he was eager to lay in a supply of the drugs that would not be available in case of war.

When Dr. Schweitzer went back to Gunsbach for a vacation in February, 1939, he sensed that war was inevitable. Desiring above all else to be with his Lambaréné people in that case, he returned at once to Africa. During the years of the war, supplies often ran short. Once, when they were virtually at an end, a large shipment came from the United States containing drugs, equipment and cooking utensils; and other shipments from America followed from time to time. Often there was a shortage of nurses at Lambaréné during this period. Madame Schweitzer once more took her turn at nursing and performed many other duties. Despite all the shortages, the hospital weathered the war years and carried on. On May 7, 1945, word came that the Armistice in Europe had been signed.

In 1948 the Schweitzers paid a memorable visit to Switzerland to visit Rhena and her husband and the four grandchildren they had never seen!

The people of the United States had long been familiar with Dr. Schweitzer, his philosophy and his hospital, through his writings and through a visit his wife and daughter had made to America in 1938. In 1939 the Albert Schweitzer Fellowship of America was formed. Dr. Schweitzer had had many invitations to visit the United States to lecture, and finally, in 1949, he came to deliver an important address in Aspen, Colorado. The occasion was the two hundredth anniversary of Goethe's birth. The people of America were drawn to this dynamic man, and the name of Schweitzer became a symbol here for greatness coupled with simplicity.

Many honors have been bestowed upon Albert Schweitzer. In countries throughout Europe he has delivered lectures on many and varied subjects. He has written books on philosophy, religion and music and on his experiences in Africa, besides his autobiography, *Out of My Life and Thought*. In recent years he has written important treatises on peace. This was also the subject of his speech in Oslo in 1954 on accepting the Nobel Peace Prize which had been awarded to him in 1952. Actually, no one knows just how many awards and prizes and degrees have been awarded Albert Schweitzer by cities, universities, and societies of philosophers, theologians, musicians and physicians. Probably never before in history has one man achieved distinction in so many fields; yet the recipient of all this acclaim remains today a simple, modest and unassuming man.

To visitors at his African hospital he presents a picture of the sincere doctor attending his black patients, the modest writer scribbling on odd pieces of paper by the light of his kerosene lamp, the musician teasing the great music of a Bach fugue from a very old, very battered piano in his bungalow.

Now an old man, still very busy, he sometimes sits beside the window at the Lambaréné mission where he can look out upon the grave of Madame Schweitzer and think back upon all that has transpired over the many years since his arrival at Lambaréné: of the Schweitzer Leper Village that was built with the Nobel Peace Prize money; of the 350-bed hospital; of the generator that now supplies electricity to the operating rooms; of the splendid staff that carries on the endless work. With all the honors that a civilized world can bestow upon a man of genius, this, his hospital in the heart of the African jungle among the people who need him, is his home. The hospital at Lambaréné is the answer to the question he asked himself as a young man: how best could he serve humanity? It is the result of his early discovery of a philosophy of living: reverence for life. The life of Albert Schweitzer, who has practiced what he believed in, is the answer to the question about man's humanity to man. It is a shining symbol of brotherhood.

Dr. Gordon S. Seagrave: Burma surgeon

In September, 1961, President John F. Kennedy sent a personal letter of commendation to Dr. Gordon S. Seagrave, who was beginning his fortieth year of service as a doctor in Namkham, Burma. President Kennedy said that Dr. Seagrave stood "as a symbol to the entire world of the American tradition of humanitarian service abroad."

Gordon Seagrave was born in Burma in 1897, the youngest of four children. His parents were Baptist missionaries and Gordon learned to speak Karen, one of the Burmese languages, before he could speak English. It was a foregone conclusion that when he grew up he, too, would be a missionary. After all, four generations of his family before him had been—to say nothing of numerous aunts and uncles.

But when he was five years old something happened which, he said, influenced him later on. A young medical missionary who was visiting the Seagraves demonstrated, to Gordon's complete astonishment, that he could drink a glass of water while standing on his head! That settled it as far as Gordon was concerned. He was filled with such admiration that he decided that someday he was going to be a medical missionary too.

Later on, the Seagraves returned to the United States and settled in Granville, Ohio. It was here that Gordon eventually was able to work his way through Denison University. Still determined to study medicine he was accepted at Johns Hopkins in Baltimore to begin his medical studies.

Of course it was necessary for him to work during the summers at whatever jobs he could find and one year he had employment at a summer camp. There he met Marion Morse whom he later married.

After graduating from Johns Hopkins, Seagrave interned at Union Memorial Hospital in Baltimore. One day when he saw the superintendent gathering up some broken-down surgical instruments that were beyond repair, Seagrave asked for them and ended up by securing a waste-basketful. It was just what he wanted! In August, 1922, Seagrave, his wife Marion and their little girl, together with the broken-down instruments, set sail for Burma.

The Seagraves were assigned to the hospital in Namkham, which is in the northern Shan States. To Seagrave this seemed almost an act of fate, for Namkham was where the young missionary had been stationed who had impressed him so many years ago with his head-standing-water-drinking abilities!

The journey to Namkham was an arduous one and the young Seagraves were exhausted when they reached there. And when they saw their hospital they felt anything but encouraged. It consisted of an almost rotten wooden building in an unbelievably filthy condition with one patient in an almost as bad state as the building. But the Seagraves knew that they must meet this challenge and that the only thing to do was to grit their teeth and get to work.

The first thing that the young doctor knew he had to do was to win the confidence of the natives. He started out with one big advantage. He could speak their language. So he began by visiting them and distributing pills where they were needed and also passing out religious tracts. He gave this up when he found out that the patients were taking in one dose all the pills he left, reasoning that if one pill helped, half a dozen would do the job quicker. And he discovered that the religious tracts which were in such demand were being welcomed as a source of paper to be used for making cigarettes.

It wasn't long before his patients began to come to him. He didn't have to seek them out. He had all kinds of surgical cases. Every night he would spend reading up on what he was going to do in the morning. While he was operating he prayed out loud and sang, which was his way of easing tension.

Early in his work at Namkham he decided that what he needed was nurses. But trained nurses were impossible to get. Then he had the idea of taking simple native girls who knew nothing of medicine and training them himself. He realized his choice of girls must be just right, for these girls would have to understand that the service they were to give was most important. It would include scrubbing floors, washing the patients' clothes and cooking their food, as well as caring for their bodily ills.

In time Seagrave's nurses became famous for their loyalty to him and he won their complete respect and affection. They called him "Daddy" and no task was too difficult or unpleasant for them to undertake. In fact, some of them would cry if he refused to let them undertake a particularly dangerous mission.

For twenty years Seagrave fought to keep his hospital going. He had what could be called a "shoe-string" budget. The foreign missionary board of the church which supported him was more enthusiastic about schools and churches than about hospitals. Many of his patients were so poor that they couldn't afford to pay. And yet there was a great need for a larger hospital. Then he heard from a Baptist church in Detroit. It wanted to establish a memorial for a former missionary who had recently died. This memorial was to be a gift of $20,000 to rebuild the hospital at Namkham. Strangely enough, the missionary was the same one who had made such an impression on the five-year-old boy so many years ago.

Everyone at Namkham pitched in to help. It was decided to build the hospital of cobblestones, as there were plenty available in the nearby river. During the daytime, coolies removed the stones from the river and left them piled up along the bank. In the evening Seagrave, his wife and the nurses would take a truck and go down to the river and bring the stones to the site of the new hospital. Seagrave did a lot of the building himself, for he wanted to show the natives that the American doctor was not ashamed to work with his hands. At his invitation, some of the missionaries stationed in other parts of the country spent their vacations in Namkham and took a hand in the building too. Eventually the hospital was completed.

Dr. Seagrave had thought he was about as busy as he could be. Besides his daily operations, his visits to patients both in Namkham and neighboring villages and his nurses' training classes, there was always an unending procession of tasks to be done. Then tragedy struck. There was an outbreak of Bubonic plague and there was little rest for him by day or night. It spread to nearby villages and even the doctor had a mild case of it himself. It was finally brought under control, but not before there had been many deaths, especially among the children. Later an outbreak of malaria among the Chinese coolies building the Burma Road brought more work, for the doctor made a trip twice a week along the length of the road to care for the sick.

In October, 1940, an event occurred which the doctor had been dreading. The Japanese had attacked China and their planes flew over northern Burma in order to reach a city in China they wanted to bomb. One day they dropped a bomb on neutral Burma in the vicinity of Namkham. The hospital was filled with casualties and Seagrave performed operations all night by candlelight.

On December 7, 1941, came the attack on Pearl Harbor. The Japanese were determined to take English-controlled Burma because of its important geographical position. Orders came for Americans to be evacuated from the country. Mrs. Seagrave, still suffering from a very severe attack of malaria, was persuaded to take their children and leave for the United States.

On three days' notice Dr. Seagrave was ordered to set up a four-hundred bed hospital back of the battle lines. The struggle for the control of Burma had already begun. The doctor was offered a commission in the British army but refused because he was afraid he would lose his American citizenship if he accepted. Then General Joseph Stilwell arrived with the American forces and Dr. Seagrave asked to have his medical unit assigned to the American fifth army.

Dr. Seagrave left some of his nurses with the British army but took the rest to the front with him. The soldiers at first could hardly believe their eyes when they saw the young girls working under the most harrowing conditions. But their amazement soon changed to the deepest admiration. The nurses were adept at setting up their operating units no matter how many Japanese bombs fell around them. They never stopped working. They worked in shifts and stayed on their feet until they nearly dropped from exhaustion. For weeks they continued with little food and little sleep. Sometimes Dr. Seagrave operated for thirty-six hours at a stretch.

Then came Stilwell's defeat and his army was forced to retreat. Operate—pack up—retreat! Day after day, that was the routine. They traveled almost constantly. Sometimes they had no food all day. The road was filled with refugees, which made it even harder. If a vehicle broke down there was no time to repair it. It had to be abandoned and those who had been using it were forced to travel on foot.

Through jungles, over mountains—the way seemed endless. Dr. Seagrave was ill with malaria and his feet were covered with sores, but he and his nurses were a source of inspiration to the rest of the company. Never complaining, always cheerful, even singing when near exhaustion, the lively, dedicated nurses kept many a "strong" soldier from giving up. And by the time they finally reached India, Seagrave and his nurses were fast becoming a legend.

Although General Stilwell had been forced to retreat he had not given up the struggle. He was determined to re-take Burma, and the new, hard-fought campaign began. Once again Seagrave and his little band of nurses joined Stilwell. Conditions seemed almost the same as on the previous march. Casualty stations had to be set up and daily the work become more strenuous. But finally Burma was recaptured and not long after, World War II was at an end.

When Dr. Seagrave returned to Namkham what a sight met his eyes! His beloved hospital was in ruins. The Japanese had used it as a headquarters and the American air force had done an excellent job of bombing it. So the rebuilding had to begin.

In 1950, new trouble came to Dr. Seagrave. And this trouble was harder to bear than that of the war years. The newly formed government of Burma was being attacked by Karen rebels. The Karens were one of the many Burmese tribes. Dr. Seagrave's main assistant was Dr. Ba Saw, who was a Karen. He joined the Karen forces, and later the Karen leader came to Namkham and demanded Dr. Ba Saw's surgical instruments and medical supplies. Dr. Seagrave gave him the instruments but only a very few medical supplies. When the news of this reached the government officials at Rangoon, they believed that Seagrave was helping the rebels.

Dr. Seagrave was arrested and thrown into prison for five months before being brought to trial. Although he had a fine defense lawyer he was found guilty. His case was appealed and later the Supreme Court of Burma acquitted him and judged him innocent of the charges of treason. Some of his friends wanted him to leave Burma and return to the United States. But Dr. Seagrave refused. He wanted but one thing—to go back to his hospital at Namkham and care for those who needed him.

The hospital at Namkham is not beautiful to look at. But beauty of surroundings does not interest Dr. Seagrave. His interest lies in his patients. He receives support from the American Medical Center for Burma, which raises funds for him. MEDICO has given him drugs, surgical supplies and cash. Drug manufacturers also send him supplies. He has about two hundred and fifty beds and fifty mats in his hospital and takes care of about twenty-five hundred hospital patients yearly as well as about ten thousand outside. He has a fine nursing school besides, and does all this on a very small budget. He takes very little salary for himself and even pays for his own food. One of his sons now manages the hospital for him and Dr. Seagrave spends his time operating, caring for the sick and teaching his nurses.

The hospital at Namkham is famous all over Burma. Its equipment is not the most modern, but patients rich and poor know that the care they receive will be of the best. Over all is the spirit of Dr. Gordon Seagrave, who has dedicated his life to his fellow men.

Thomas A. Dooley:
doctor, educator, humanitarian

Tom Dooley, son of a well-to-do St. Louis family, was born January 17, 1927. When young Tom was a student at Notre Dame, no one ever dreamed that one day his name would be known throughout the entire United States. Nor could anyone have foreseen that it would be revered not only by citizens of his own country but by thousands of Asians as well.

Although Tom had few worries when he was growing up, cars to ride in, a college education and finally medical school, he always seemed to have the desire to help those more unfortunate than himself. Even when he was a boy he would bring home maimed or neglected pets and try to cure them. When he was older he would visit the home for neglected boys in St. Louis and get permission to take the boys to art galleries and museums.

In medical school, his professors thought he was probably destined to be a society doctor. But Tom had other plans and upon graduation he volunteered for duty as a United States Navy doctor. He was commissioned as a Lieutenant, jg, in the Navy Medical Corps and attached to the unit of Dr. Julius Anderson, head of the Preventive Medical Unit in Haiphong.

Haiphong is in Southeast Asia just north of the border which separates South Vietnam from North Vietnam. To understand what was happening in Haiphong in 1954 when young Dr. Tom Dooley arrived there, it is necessary to know a little of the history of the country of Vietnam. Vietnam had been one of the three former French Indo-China Associated States located just south of China and east of the countries of Cambodia and Laos. During World War II, Vietnam was occupied by the Japanese. At the end of the war in

1945, the Communists in Vietnam tried to seize the government. France opposed this and from 1945 to 1954 there was fighting between the French and the Communists. In July, 1954, a cease-fire agreement was finally signed in Geneva, Switzerland.

According to this agreement Vietnam was to be divided. The Communists were given control of the northern part of the country and the southern part was to be for the non-Communists. In 1955, South Vietnam became a republic and elected a president.

In the treaty signed at Geneva in 1954, it was also agreed that any non-Communist living in North Vietnam would be permitted to leave and to migrate to South Vietnam. It wasn't expected that many would want to give up their homes and leave. But freedom is precious and hundreds of thousands of persons living in North Vietnam chose to abandon their homes and to seek new ones in a non-Communist state. This meant that most of the refugees would pass through Haiphong.

Tom Dooley's first assignment in the Navy was the job of building refugee camps in Haiphong to provide humanitarian and medical attention for any of the refugees who needed it. Dr. Dooley afterward said that although he had taken many courses in medical school, "How to build a refugee camp" was not one of them! But one doesn't argue with a superior officer who issues an order, so he set out to accomplish his task.

Normally, Haiphong had a population of about one hundred thousand but with all the refugees pouring in, at times this number was doubled. Dooley's job entailed building a tent city which could accommodate a shifting population of between ten thousand and fifteen thousand persons.

When he went into Haiphong he found that most of the refugees were living in the streets and gutters with no sanitary provisions of any kind. The first thing he had to do was find a place to build a camp. He finally decided on a spot about four miles from town. Tents were flown in from Japan and his workers were French Moroccan soldiers and Chinese coolies.

After several days of hard work the tent city was ready for occupancy. One section was reserved for the hospital area. It wasn't long before he was treating hundreds of patients for diseases he had heard of only by reading about them in books.

Medical supplies were in great demand. American ships anchored in nearby waters gave all they could spare but it was not nearly enough. So Dr. Dooley began writing letters to American drug companies for help. And they all responded most generously. The drug companies were not the only ones who answered his request. Others donated such items as soap and other needed articles.

As Dr. Dooley and his assistants administered drugs and bound up wounds they said, "This is American aid." For they knew that Communist propaganda had been informing the poor refugees that the Americans were a selfish people interested only in securing wealth for themselves. Many of the refugees were grateful, but many were suspicious of the Americans. Some believed what they had been told—that the inoculations they were being given were filled with germs. Sometimes patients were so frightened that they would physically injure those who were trying to help them.

After treating those who were sick, vaccinating all of them and de-lousing them to free them of vermin, Dr. Dooley and his aides saw that the refugees were put on board ships that would take them farther south.

More refugees came in daily. The American commander who was in charge of the refugee operation was recalled to Japan and Dr. Dooley was left to take over his duties. It was not easy. The average working day was about sixteen hours. Conditions at times seemed to get worse instead of improving; but, discouraged as he occasionally was, Dr. Dooley never wanted to give up. He had discovered that he had found the purpose of his life. It was to serve others.

Finally the last of the refugees left camp and the Communists began to come in. Dr. Dooley's tour of duty with the Navy was completed and he returned to the United States. He could have settled down and established himslf in his own medical practice. But he wasn't contented. He knew what he had to do. He wanted to return to Asia, though not to Vietnam. The north of that country belonged to the Communists and already medical teams had been set up and were operating in the south. So he decided to talk to the Laotian Ambassador to the United States and see if he could set up a medical unit in Laos.

At first the Ambassador didn't believe he was serious. But finally he realized that this young doctor meant it when he said he wanted to help those in need of medical attention and he agreed to do all he could. He told Dr. Dooley among other things, that in Laos, which had a population of two million people, there was only one doctor qualified to be called that by western standards. For the most part the people relied on witch doctors and sorcerers.

Getting permission to go to Laos and getting prepared to go were two different matters. A mission such as he planned must have backing to give it official status; so first of all Dr. Dooley talked to those in charge of the International Rescue Committee and arranged to come under its protection. This organization, through its work for those in need, had gained respect throughout the world. But Dr. Dooley was to finance his own mission. His next consideration, necessarily, was to secure needed funds.

He had the royalties from his book *Deliver Us from Evil,* which he had written on his return from Vietnam. And then there were the proceeds from a lecture tour he had made. But much more would be needed. Remembering the good luck he had had when he appealed to the drug companies for help, he again made the rounds. Drug companies, surgical supply houses and those carrying equipment such as stoves and lanterns came to his aid. Some gave supplies outright; some sold them to him at a fraction of their cost. Even the United States Navy helped, for it transported all his supplies and equipment even though he was now a civilian.

Finally he had the important task of choosing the right men to accompany him and then persuading them to go. His choices were Norman Baker, Peter Kessey and Dennis Shepard, three of the enlisted men who had helped him at Vietnam. Dr. Dooley's persuasive powers were great, for though it meant personal sacrifices for all of them they agreed to help him. In July, 1956, with his assistants, he went back to Asia.

Dr. Dooley had wanted to set up his unit at Nam Tha but neither the United States Ambassador to Laos nor the Laotian authorities wanted him to, for Nam Tha was too close to the border of Communist China. Instead, he was advised to go to Vang Vieng about one hundred and twenty miles north of the Laotian capital and quite far south of China. During the Indo-China war Vang Vieng had been in the hands of the Communists and he was told that conditions there were in a bad state.

Even though he thought he was prepared for what he would find in Vang Vieng, Dooley could never have imagined the primitive health conditions he saw there. Even the house he and his assistants were to live in was in a state of disrepair. It was a typical Laotian hut set up on stilts six feet off the ground and could be reached only by means of a ladder. But the people gave the young Americans a welcome reception. They had heard of their coming and as soon as Dooley and his assistants were unpacked they were in business. From the very first day, long lines of people waited patiently to get treatment from the doctor. Soon he was making calls to the neighboring countryside in his jeep to see those too sick to be brought into the village.

So much of the disease in Vang Vieng was caused through ignorance of simple health rules that every night in addition to the Walt Disney movies which were shown in their front yard, the staff took turns in lecturing to the people on how to improve their everyday living habits. Of course these lectures were delivered through a native interpreter who was very proud of his job.

There was another thing for which Dr. Dooley was quite unprepared. He found that his "sick call" line was not limited to people but often included a sick horse or a water buffalo that someone would bring along for treatment!

One of Tom Dooley's main ideas was that it was not wise to set up a medical station as a permanent American outpost. Rather, it should be set up in such a way that the natives themselves eventually could take over. With this thought in mind he began to train people he considered capable of caring for the sick. He had classes for nurses and instructed them in the basic rules of health. Whenever he assisted at the birth of a baby he took one or two of his nurses along so he could show them the importance of proper care of the mother and child.

In January, 1957, when he thought that the natives could do a better job of taking care of themselves than they had before, he went back to the capital and had an interview with the Minister of Health. Dooley explained to him that he would be able to stay in Laos only about four more months, as his funds were limited.

The Minister of Health was amazed, because he had thought that the United States Government was financing the Dooley operation. So he made the doctor an offer. The Laos government would provide the facilities for work, the army would transport the supplies, the Ministry of Education would help with the educational part of the program and the government would pay the Laotian members of his staff, if Dr. Dooley would stay longer in Laos. Tom Dooley couldn't resist this offer. Somehow he would manage. Once more he asked if he could set up his station at Nam Tha, which had been denied him before. As tensions in that part of the country had eased somewhat, he was granted this request.

One of the American members of Dooley's team decided to go back home as he had planned but two agreed to stay with him. He immediately secured two new volunteers, both of whom were students at Notre Dame, his Alma Mater. After they had arrived in Laos the group set out for Nam Tha.

They found Nam Tha a larger and more progressive town than Vang Vieng, and their living quarters there were better, too. Here they had a regular house—although they shared it with a telegraph office, the telegraph operator and his large family and two young school teachers!

The first task was to fix up a building for a hospital. They were given one large enough so that they could have a dispensary as well as an isolation ward. At first, cases came in fast, as they had in Vang Vieng. Then they dwindled away, and Tom and his assistants soon found out the answer. The local witch doctors had put a "hex" on the hospital and no one dared to enter. So the Americans decided to adopt the old slogan, "If you can't like 'em, join 'em!" They began treating the witch doctors as colleagues. After Dooley's men had dispensed the drugs they would call on the witch doctors to invoke the spirits. It pleased the witch doctors to see how their patients recovered and they quickly lifted the "hex" on the hospital.

Once again Dr. Dooley began the same methods of education he had used in Vang Vieng. Classes were held in the treatment of the sick and the proper care of children. People were eager to learn. After all, no one wants to be sick and parents are the same the world over. They love their children and want to see them well and happy. Dr. Dooley knew that most health problems are due to ignorance and that persons who don't understand them accept disease as normal. It was necessary to teach the people to take care of themselves.

When he felt that the people in Nam Tha could take over, he decided that the time had come to leave. It was because he had such firm convictions on this matter that he always tried to keep everything as simple as possible. There were no X-ray or other delicate machines installed. The only drugs left were those which native nurses could be taught to use safely. But when he finally left he had the promise of the Minister of Health that the hospital would have a charter, that nurses would be sent to Nam Tha and that a doctor would replace him. In return he promised to leave all of his equipment in addition to $25,000 worth of medicine.

After leaving Laos, Dr. Dooley returned to the United States. He was very anxious that an organization be set up to carry forward the work he had started. He wanted American medical aid for countries that needed it, but he believed it should be free of government control. Rather he thought it should be on a person-to-person basis. According to his plan, the doctors would be visitors. Small hospitals would be built and stocked, the doctors would train the villagers to run them themselves, and then they would move on somewhere else.

Once again Dr. Tom Dooley approached the International Rescue Committee, which decided to amend its charter so that it could accept the task of providing medical aid to parts of the world which needed it. This part of its work came to be known as MEDICO.

Later on, Dr. Dooley went back to Laos under the sponsorship of MEDICO, and at the suggestion of the Laotian government went to Muong Sing to establish another hospital with the help of two other young Americans.

Shortly after this, trouble came to Laos. The Communists from North Vietnam provided Communists in Laos with uniforms, arms and ammunition. Danger surrounded the newly founded hospital and Dr. Dooley was faced with the choice of abandoning that hospital or staying. He decided to stay, but then a personal tragedy intervened. He discovered that he had cancer and was forced to come back to the United States for an operation. This was about the middle of August, 1959.

Even though he knew his illness was serious, it didn't stop him. Barely out of the hospital, he lectured to raise more money for his hospital projects. In the meantime he had written two more books, *The Edge of Tomorrow* and *The Night They Burned the Mountain*. Royalties from these books were turned over to MEDICO. He received the Criss Award, a ten thousand dollar prize from the Mutual

Insurance Company of Omaha, for his outstanding devotion to the cause of bringing medical aid to millions of people throughout the world. This, too, he gave to the cause that was dear to him.

Although Dr. Tom Dooley returned to Laos to continue his work, it was not for long. Fatally ill, he managed to stay as long as his strength endured, and then he was flown to New York to re-enter a hospital. On January 17, 1961, Tom Dooley was thirty-four years old. On January 18 he was claimed by death.

Dr. Tom Dooley was admired and loved by hundreds of thousands of people. The "beautiful American" was the name by which he was known to some, but there were others who criticized him. Some doctors felt that his ideas of teaching the people to carry on by themselves would keep the quality of medical service too low. Tom Dooley's reply to that was that at least it was better than it had been before.

Some said the methods he used were outdated by at least a century. He didn't mind admitting this was true but said they were at least three or four centuries ahead of what was being used before he came.

Criticized for the appearance of his hospitals, he said that the natives would feel strange in a gleaming white hospital such as Americans were used to, and probably wouldn't come at all.

As always happens when a person has push and drive and definite ideas, Tom Dooley incurred the hostility of some, but many more loved and respected him and were grateful for what he did. Certainly his personal courage in the face of what he knew was an early death was something to be marveled at and admired. And he made the word "American" a word of honor in many parts of the world.

After Dr. Dooley's death the Dr. Tom Dooley Foundation was organized by a group of persons, including Tom's mother, his brother and some of the doctors who worked with him in Asia, who have dedicated themselves to carrying on his work on a personal basis.

When they started they had two projects, one an orphanage in Saigon and the other a Tibetan refugee program which was started before Dr. Dooley's death—the sending of two mobile health units to northern India to take care of refugees coming in from China.

Tom Dooley's name will be remembered for many years to come.

He was a man of vision and compassion. He believed firmly that medical aid is one of the most important tools used in building the foundation of world peace because it recognizes no barrier of race or creed. What it does recognize is what Dr. Tom Dooley believed in with all his heart—the brotherhood of man.

Ship of Hope:
health opportunity for people everywhere

On September 22, 1960, a great white ship sailed out of San Francisco harbor bound for Southeast Asia. It was the S.S. *Hope I,* a hospital ship equipped for her first mission, taking medical and technical assistance to countries where it was greatly needed. She was well named, for to many thousands of people she would bring hope where there had been despair. Where had she come from, this ship, and what was her story?

Behind every great project there must first be an idea. This one began with a Washington, D.C., physician, Dr. William B. Walsh, founder and president of Project Hope: the People-to-People Health Foundation, Incorporated. His plan was to create a Great White Fleet of hospital ships that would visit friendly countries in need of medical help. Supported by the American people, outside the government, it would serve many thousands in other lands. In other words, it was to be a people-to-people program in the truest sense of the word.

The nonprofit organization was incorporated in December, 1958, and immediately Dr. Walsh began to work toward the accomplishment of the project's purpose. Dr. Walsh found out that a navy ship, the *Consolation,* docked in San Francisco, was no longer in use. It had been built during the Second World War and had last seen service in Korea. He explained his plan to President Eisenhower, with the result that the navy vessel was loaned to the organization as ship number one in the proposed fleet. Next, the American President Lines offered to operate her at cost; but money, much money, was needed. For a year, appeals were made to labor, business, industry and private individuals, and a sum of more than three million dollars was raised. Pharmaceutical and drug supply companies donated medicine and equipment. The project moved on to a successful conclusion for the launching of the first ship.

When the S.S. *Hope* pulled out of San Francisco bound for Indonesia she was well fitted out with the most modern equipment, supplies and training aids that could be obtained. Her staff consisted of volunteers from the medical field who had donated a year of their time and skills: fifteen doctors, two dentists, twenty-five nurses and thirty auxiliary personnel. Besides these there was a rotating staff of thirty-five volunteer physicians who would be flown to the ship at various ports for periods of two to four months.

The hospital ship was a veritable floating medical center, an answer to any physician's dream. There were three operating rooms in addition to a special one for eye surgery, and also a maternity delivery room; there were beds for two hundred and fifty patients; there was a medical library; there was the best equipment that modern medicine can offer. Furthermore, the ship could boast of a system for making drinking water, *and milk,* out of sea water. One of the great needs in the countries that would be visited would be milk for the children. This machine, from dried products, would produce thousands of gallons of milk daily, with a system of bottling it in paper containers.

And so the S.S. *Hope* went out on its first voyage of twenty-two days and twenty thousand miles to its first port, Djakarta, the capital of Indonesia. The fifteen-ton white ship, bedecked with flags, must have been a welcome sight to the people who were eagerly awaiting her at the dock.

Just how welcome can be better understood when one realizes the sore need for medical aid in that place. In the United States there is one doctor for approximately nine hundred persons, and a total of seventy medical schools. But in all of Indonesia, with its three thousand islands and eighty-two million people, there are only two medical schools. It is estimated that there is one doctor for every ten thousand persons—and in some areas only one doctor to a half million people. By ancient custom the natives go to the village medicine man when there is illness. Disease is believed to come from evil spirits. The doctors and nurses of Indonesia must constantly fight ignorance and superstition and try to overcome the harm that is done by the medicine men.

When the S.S. *Hope* had docked at Djakarta, her first visitors were the ambassadors to Indonesia from many countries, including Russia. Also, a welcome group waiting to come aboard were the rotating doctors who had flown to Djakarta, to take part in the intensive work that must be done. These were joined by Indonesian doctors who would work side by side with the American physicians.

Finally, the patients came aboard in all stages of illness or disease, some of them close to death. And now the real work of the hospital ship began. Everyone on shipboard had the conviction that the S.S. *Hope* would be a success, and each one worked hard to make that conviction come true. Operating rooms were in constant use day after day and night after night. Thousands were treated. Thousands went off the ship with new hope, some with new sight, some with restored hearing, all with gratitude that only those with the prospect of a new and better life can feel. To them the ship was like a gift from God.

But the treatment that was given by the doctors and nurses was not the only good that came from the white hospital ship, for the ultimate purpose of Project Hope was to teach. The Indonesian doctors and technicians who worked side by side with the skilled Americans were discovering wonderful things. New techniques and medical skills were learned and could be taught to others in this land where so much learning was needed. For weeks, the Indonesian doctors observed and studied and discussed cases with the American physicians. They were eager for knowledge. An Indonesian writer once said, "The East forgets many things, but will never forget its teachers."

One of the great satisfactions of those who were working on Project Hope was to learn that the Indonesians were planning to equip a hospital ship of their own which would travel to their many islands to treat and to teach their own people how to care for the sick and diseased.

Those who were on the S.S. *Hope* during its stay in Indonesia had the opportunity to realize fully what this people-to-people program meant to those who were treated. In a letter to Dr. Walsh, Father

John F. Magner, the Catholic Chaplain, told how the staff had fallen in love with the children of Indonesia. He wrote: "Had we come looking for any human reward for our mission, we have received it a thousandfold." The small patients had good cause to remember Father Magner. Every day he visited the children's wards and took those who could walk on a tour of the ship. These tours had a joyful ending for the little ones, for they always ended up at the canteen where the Father bought them all American ice cream sodas!

The children's ward of the *Hope* was truly a place to delight the children who were patients there. The walls were brightly painted by one of the nurses with pictures of all kinds of animals. Handiwork of the nurses also were the pretty smocks worn by the children, gaily embroidered with ships and toys. There were lots of real toys for the little ones to play with, sent as gifts from the American people.

One of the small patients while the ship was in Indonesia was little Hansje Enam, a five-year-old boy from the island of Sumbawa. The lad had had cataracts on both eyes since he was three, causing total blindness. A surgeon removed both cataracts. One day after the operation, before Hansje had recovered his sight, a nurse picked him up from his bed in the children's ward and held him in her arms. He felt her class pin, which was shaped like an oak leaf. She said her name for him, "Sister Nancy." (Nurses are called "Sister" in Indonesia.) The next day when she again picked him up, he felt her pin and said, "Sister Nancy." Later on, the nurse heard him talking in his native tongue to one of the Indonesian nurses. "What did he say?" she asked. And the nurse told her that Hansje had said, "That is Sister Nancy and she is very kind to me."

One night the nurse took Hansje on deck. She saw him looking up at the sky and suddenly he said *"Bulan"* which means "moon." Then she knew that he was regaining his sight. When the time came for Hansje to go back to shore, he sat on the nurse's lap and squinted at the brightness of the sun. And as the launch drew away from the S.S. *Hope* he pointed to the ship, saying, *"Kapal Hope putih."* ("The *Hope* ship is white.")

The S.S. *Hope* visits only those countries that have requested it, and enough requests have been received to keep the hospital ship busy for years to come. As she and sister ships now being planned sail across the seas to other lands, the entire world will see that the people of the United States are truly concerned about their neighbors. On every bottle of medicine that is given out by the medical staff of the ship there is a sentence printed on the label: "The people of the United States wish you well." The sentiment is backed by the deeds performed by Project Hope.

part V

THE UNITED NATIONS

THE UNITED NATIONS

*Come, my friends, 'tis not too late
to seek a newer world.*

—ALFRED TENNYSON

United Nations: instrument of peace

Even before World War II was over, the problem of how to bring peace to the world and maintain it was the concern of many people. Two world wars had brought terrible destruction to many countries, ruining their economies, destroying their homes and, worst of all, killing and maiming their citizens. Another war was unthinkable. Modern methods of warfare with new inventions of destruction, if continued, could very well set the world back thousands of years. In order for the peoples of the world to progress, a new world order was imperative. Never before in history was the practice of brotherhood so badly needed; never before was there a time when it was so necessary for nations to learn to live together in peace.

The leaders of the Allied Powers of the war saw this great need and they envisioned an organization that would embrace all nations in a common aim: to maintain peace through arbitration without the use of arms. It was their thoughts and concern over this matter that led to the United Nations. The League of Nations had been established after World War I, but it had failed. A new start must be made.

On August 21, 1944, while bitter fighting was taking place on French soil in the invasion of enemy-occupied France, an important meeting was held at Dumbarton Oaks in Washington, D.C. Attending were representatives of the Big Four, consisting of the United States, Great Britain, Russia and China. During the conference which lasted until October 7, the structure of the United Nations was laid. The first step accomplished, it was agreed to have a conference later in San Francisco.

The San Francisco Conference met April 25, 1945, with representatives of fifty-one nations attending. A charter was drawn up and on June 24 was signed by fifty nations. (Poland signed it later.)

The Charter of the United Nations is so important a document that a portion of it is included here.

We the people of the United Nations

Determined to save succeeding generations from the scourge of war . . .

To reaffirm faith in fundamental human rights, in the dignity and worth of the human person, in the equal right of men and women and of nations large and small, and

To establish . . . justice and respect for international law and

To promote social progress and better standards of life in larger freedom, and for these ends

To practice tolerance and live together in peace with one another as good neighbors, and

To unite our strength to maintain international peace and security, and

To insure . . . that armed force shall not be used, save in the common interest, and

To employ international machinery for the . . . advancement of all peoples

Have resolved to combine our efforts to accomplish these aims.

THE ORGANS OF THE UNITED NATIONS

To achieve its purpose, six principal organs were created. The most important of these is the *General Assembly*. All members are represented in it and all have the privilege of speaking on any subject which falls within the charter. Managing the financial affairs of the entire organization is a part of its duties. Recommendations are made by the General Assembly to other branches of the U.N. The Assembly is required to meet once a year and also at other times in case of emergency. Two examples of special emergency sessions were those held in the spring of 1947 to act on the war in Palestine and in 1956 in the Suez Canal crisis. Both of these international disputes were settled by the U.N. through negotiation, proving to the world that the United Nations was effective as an instrument of peace.

The Security Council is the organ that has the most power because the member nations mutually agree to carry out whatever decisions the Council makes. The Council investigates any situation which might lead to war and tries to settle disputes through arbitration or other peaceful methods but, as a last resort, has the authority to assemble troops to be sent to the troubled area. Of the eleven members of the Security Council, five are permanent: the United States, the Soviet Union, Great Britain, France and China (still represented by the Chinese Nationalists of Chiang Kai-shek, with headquarters on Formosa). The other six members are elected by the General Assembly to serve two-year terms. The Council is in almost continuous session. It works very closely with the General Assembly. When emergencies arise, it can call a special session of the General Assembly. The General Assembly makes recommendations which are acted upon by the Security Council.

The Economic and Social Council, or ECOSOC as it is often called, concerns itself with problems of economic and social nature, such as full employment and higher standards of living for all people. It has many commissions and committees that carry on investigations and studies and then make recommendations to the General Assembly. ECOSOC has eighteen commissions that deal with such important matters as Employment, Transportation and Communications, Human Rights, Status of Women, Population, World Health, Statistics and Technical Assistance. These commissions and the specialized agencies within them constitute the greatest international organization that has ever been created to solve the social and economic problems that beset the world. The Economic and Social Council is one of the U.N.'s busiest and most active organs.

The Trusteeship Council is concerned with trust territories that are placed under its jurisdiction. Some of these are countries that were born as a result of breaking away from other countries. Others, placed under the guardianship of the United Nations, are called Non-Self-Governing Territories because they are governed by other countries. Some who were originally under the Trusteeship Council have already gained their independence and others will eventually do so. The Council is composed of fourteen member nations, seven of whom are given the authority to govern the areas that come under the Council's jurisdiction. One of the duties of the Council is to examine and consider the petitions and grievances that come to it from the Trust Territories. In other words, the Trusteeship Council is guardian and governor for those new countries that are struggling to achieve independence.

The International Court of Justice is made up of fifteen judges, all of different nationalities, with headquarters at The Hague, Netherlands. It is the legal arm of the United Nations. Every U.N. member is automatically a member of the Court and may refer cases to it for settlement. However, when two nations are in dispute, both must agree to submit the case to the Court before the case can be considered by it. If the case is then heard, the nations involved must abide by the Court's decision. Questions involving international laws, treaties and obligations, as well as boundary disputes, are settled in this way by the Court. The decisions handed down by the International Court of Justice have been the means of preventing many dangerous situations between countries.

The Secretariat is headed by the most important member of the United Nations, the Secretary-General. Either he or one of his deputies must be present at every meeting of the General Assembly, the Security Council and the Trusteeship Council. He makes an annual report to the General Assembly on all phases of the work of the United Nations. One of his duties is to bring to the attention of the Security Council any matter that is a threat to international peace and security. There are eight departments in the Secretariat, each headed by an Assistant Secretary-General. All the members of the Secretariat must take an oath of allegiance to the United Nations. While delegates to the U.N. are influenced by the interests of their representative countries, the Secretariat must pledge their first loyalty to the United Nations.

The Secretary-General has come to be recognized as the leader of the United Nations. The first was Trygve Lie of Norway, who served his first term from 1946 to 1951 and then was re-elected and served until 1953. He was succeeded by Dag Hammarskjold, Swedish diplomat, who served until his death on September 18, 1961. He was killed in a plane crash while on a mission of the United Nations seeking a cease-fire between U.N. and Katangan Forces in the Congo. U Thant of Burma was elected Acting Secretary-General on November 3, 1961.

THE HEADQUARTERS OF THE UNITED NATIONS

The thousands of persons who serve at the U.N. have the advantage of working in one of the most beautiful groups of buildings in the world. New York City was chosen for the headquarters when the

United Nations was first organized. The site, an eighteen-acre plot of ground between Forty-second and Forty-eighth Streets in Manhattan, overlooks the East River. The land was once occupied by the Algonquin Indians and was purchased from them more than three hundred years ago by Peter Minuit, who later became Governor of New Netherland (New York). The land for the Headquarters was purchased with money given to the United Nations by John D. Rockefeller. Money for the buildings came from many nations, each donating a share in proportion to the size of the country. When the Headquarters Agreement was signed by the United Nations and the United States, the boundary lines became international boundary lines and the land came into the possession of nations around the world. Also the United Nations became an official geographic and postal address: United Nations, N.Y.

Building began in 1948. On October 24, 1949 (U.N. Day), the cornerstone was laid. On it the words "United Nations" were inscribed in English, French, Chinese, Russian and Spanish. In May, 1951, the temporary headquarters at Lake Success were abandoned and the organization, except for the General Assembly, moved into its beautiful new permanent home. The first meeting of the General Assembly in the new Headquarters took place the following year.

The Headquarters consist of three main buildings. The tall skyscraper is the Secretariat Building. The two low buildings are the General Assembly and the Conference Building. In the plaza before the tall Secretariat, there is a fountain which was given by American school children as a token of friendship to children of nations around the world. Close to it is a children's playground. The thirty-nine story Secretariat is a very busy place, for it is occupied by about three thousand people. Besides the hundreds of office rooms where the Secretariat members do their work, there are rooms for newspaper, radio and television reporters. There are also rooms for the numerous translators and interpreters who are in constant demand at this many-nation, multi-language organization. It is on the thirty-eighth floor of this building that the Secretary-General has his offices. Also within this large edifice, making it really a city-within-a-city, there are a post office, a fire department, a printing and binding department, a cafeteria, drugstore, gift shop and other departments necessary to the smooth-running operation of the vast machinery of the U.N.

The General Assembly Building contains a circular auditorium with rows of desks in the pit for the delegates and two large balconies for the spectators. A rostrum for speakers faces the delegates' seats, and behind it there are three seats on a raised platform. Here sit the President of the Assembly, the Secretary-General and his Executive Assistant. Behind them on the wall is the familiar blue U.N. emblem, a map of the world surrounded by olive branches. The interpreters sit in small booths set into the wall at the rear of the delegates. They have very important work to do. They listen to the speakers and translate the speeches immediately into a different language. Each speech is translated into the five official languages of the United Nations: English, French, Russian, Chinese and Spanish. Each delegate from the different countries can put on the headphone attached to his chair, dial into the language he wishes to hear, and understand exactly what the speaker is saying.

The Conference Building is connected to the General Assembly by long passageways. The main part of this building consists of three large conference rooms where meetings are held by the Security Council, the Economic and Social Council and the Trusteeship Council. These rooms were designed by Scandinavian architects and are very impressive. The plan of each conference room is similar to the large General Assembly auditorium and similarly equipped with headphones and translator booths.

The Dag Hammarskjold Library was dedicated as a memorial to the much-loved Secretary-General on September 16, 1961. A gift of the Ford Foundation, the Library has six stories and a penthouse, with three additional floors underground. It has space for four hundred thousand volumes and contains an auditorium and rooms for special sections. The building is connected to the Secretariat by a glass passageway.

Hundreds of thousands of visitors pass through the U.N. buildings each year. A feeling of confidence in this great organization should be inspired by what they see. All about them are people of different-colored skins speaking in different tongues, making it apparent that the success of the United Nations is due not to any one person or any one nation but to many persons from many nations. One of Dag Hammarskjold's projects while he was serving as Secretary-General was a Meditation Room where anyone who wished could sit and relax, meditate or pray. It may be that the thoughts and prayers in that room have influenced and will continue to influence the world's destiny for good.

The United Nations may not be perfect and it may not yet have attained all its original ideals of purpose, but it is by far the most effective step that has ever been taken to unify nations and to keep them working toward a better world.

The Declaration of Human Rights

The Declaration of Human Rights, expressed in simple, understandable language, explains in detail what the Preamble to the Charter of the United Nations describes as one of the purposes of that organization.

After stating as its first goal the saving of mankind from the scourge of war, it continues: "To reaffirm faith in fundamental human rights, in the dignity and worth of the human person, in the equal right of men and women and of nations large and small . . ."

The United States delegation to that first United Nations meeting in San Francisco, in 1945, was well aware of the importance of such a statement as this. The first ten amendments to the Constitution of the United States, known as the "Bill of Rights," were added because the citizens of the newly-founded republic felt they were necessary as a safeguard to their rights. So it is not surprising that our delegation, with the support of others, requested that there be included in the Charter of the United Nations a provision for setting up a commission to write a Declaration of Human Rights. As a result of this request, Chapter X, Article 62 of the Charter, in explaining the functions of the Economic and Social Council of the United Nations, states, "It may make recommendations for the purpose of promoting respect for and observance of, human rights and fundamental freedoms for all."

With the granting of this authority, the Economic and Social Council, soon after its organization, appointed a commission to work on a Declaration that would be acceptable to the General Assembly of the United Nations. One of the members appointed was Mrs. Eleanor Roosevelt and when the commission met for its first session she was elected chairman and continued in that position until the Declaration was completed. Soon after its first meeting, the commission recommended that it should be composed of eighteen members. There would be one each from the United States, the Soviet Union, the United Kingdom, France and Nationalist China. The other thirteen members were to rotate from other member states of the United Nations.

The commission began its work in the spring of 1946 and held its first meetings in a classroom of Hunter College in New York City. Its first problem was to decide just what form the Declaration should have. It finally decided that it would write an International Bill of Rights which would be divided into three parts:

PART 1.   A declaration which would define human rights, including not only political and civil rights but also social, economic and cultural rights.

PART 2.   A covenant or agreement in treaty form concerning these rights, which could be signed by the nations accepting them. They could then be made a part of international law.

PART 3.   Machinery to enforce these rights after they had been made into law.

The reason underlying the necessity for Part 2 was that although the General Assembly might approve the resolutions expressed in Part 1, no resolutions passed by the General Assembly are legally binding on its members.

The writing of Part 1, the Declaration of Human Rights, was not an easy task. In fact it took two years of hard work to accomplish it. Every word had to be chosen carefully so that in translation its meaning would not be changed. And even then it sometimes resulted that various interpretations could be given to the same phrase. Each article had to be debated pro and con, back and forth, until it was in a form acceptable to all members of the commission.

The final meetings of the commission concerned with writing the

Declaration were held in Geneva, Switzerland, in 1947. In order to get it completed in the time the commission had allotted itself, it was necessary to hold meetings at night as well as in the daytime. On December 17 the work was finally completed and ready to submit to the General Assembly.

In 1948, when the General Assembly met in Paris, the Declaration of Human Rights was presented for its approval. It came under a great deal of debate but when the vote was finally taken it was accepted without a dissenting vote. However, there were a few countries which abstained from voting at all.

In reading through the Declaration of Human Rights it is interesting to see how much of it sounds familiar to us.

Its first Article states, "All human beings are born free and equal in dignity and rights." In our own Declaration of Independence we read, "We hold these truths to be self-evident, that all men are created equal, that they are endowed by their Creator with certain unalienable Rights . . ."

Article 3 of the Declaration of Human Rights states, "Every one has the right to life, liberty and security of person." Our Declaration of Independence says, ". . . that among these (rights) are Life, Liberty and the pursuit of Happiness." And all of us are familiar with the words of Abraham Lincoln's famous Gettysburg address, "Fourscore and seven years ago our Fathers brought forth on this continent a new nation, conceived in liberty and dedicated to the proposition that all men are created equal."

Other articles in the Declaration of Human Rights state the same thoughts, if not in the same words, as expressed in the first ten amendments of our Constitution, such as the right of persons to fair trial and the prohibition of cruel punishment. And in Article 25 it defines the right of living standards which include food, clothing, housing and medical care.

Article 4 of the Declaration states that "No one shall be held in slavery or servitude." The Thirteenth Amendment to our Constitution abolished slavery in the United States.

Articles 18 and 19 of the Declaration deal with the rights of freedom of religion and expression of opinion. On January 6, 1941, in a speech to Congress, President Franklin D. Roosevelt gave what he considered four basic freedoms:

1. Freedom of speech and expression
2. Freedom to worship
3. Freedom from want
4. Freedom from fear

These freedoms were expressed again when President Roosevelt and Prime Minister Churchill issued the Atlantic Charter seeking "Assurance that all men in all the lands may live out their lives in freedom from fear and want."

Although the Declaration was accepted by the General Assembly in 1948, the work of the commission has continued. Because of the many questions involved in the Declaration, a single treaty covering all the points seemed impossible to achieve. So it was decided to write two. One was to cover the civil and political rights. The other was to cover social, economic and cultural rights. At each meeting of the General Assembly the debate on the articles has continued. Although the way to total acceptance seems long and sometimes discouraging, the influence of the Declaration has been great.

Since its completion there have been many new states formed in the world, especially in Africa. Many of the principles of the Declaration have been included in their constitutions. Its articles also are being used as standards to be achieved by other established governments. In the ideals it expresses one cannot help but feel that probably it is the greatest of all human documents.

THE DECLARATION OF HUMAN RIGHTS

ARTICLE 1.   All human beings are born free and equal in dignity and rights. They are endowed with reason and conscience and should act towards one another in a spirit of brotherhood.

ARTICLE 2.   Everyone is entitled to all the rights and freedoms set forth in this Declaration, without distinction of any kind such as race, color, sex, language, religion, political or other opinion, national or social origin, property, birth or other social status.

Furthermore, no distinction shall be made on the basis of the political, jurisdictional or international status of the country or territory to which a person belongs, whether it be independent, trust, non-selfgoverning or under any other limitation of sovereignty.

ARTICLE 3. Everyone has the right to life, liberty and security of person.

ARTICLE 4. No one shall be held in slavery or servitude; slavery and the slave trade shall be prohibited in all their forms.

ARTICLE 5. No one shall be subjected to torture or to cruel, inhuman or degrading treatment or punishment.

ARTICLE 6. Everyone has the right to recognition everywhere as a person before the law.

ARTICLE 7. All are equal before the law and are entitled without any discrimination to equal protection of the law. All are entitled to equal protection against any discrimination in violation of this Declaration and against any incitement to such discrimination.

ARTICLE 8. Everyone has the right to an effective remedy by the competent national tribunals for acts violating the fundamental rights granted him by the constitution or by law.

ARTICLE 9. No one shall be subjected to arbitrary arrest, detention or exile.

ARTICLE 10. Everyone is entitled in full equality to a fair and public hearing by an independent and impartial tribunal, in the determination of his rights and obligations and of any criminal charge against him.

ARTICLE 11. (1) Everyone charged with a penal offense has the right to be presumed innocent until proved guilty according to law in a public trial at which he has had all the guarantees necessary for his defense.
(2) No one shall be held guilty of any penal offense on account of any act or admission which did not constitute a penal offense, under national or international law, at the time when it was committed. Nor shall a heavier penalty be imposed

than the one that was applicable at the time the penal offense was committed.

ARTICLE 12.   No one shall be subjected to arbitrary interference with his privacy, family, home or correspondence, nor to attacks upon his honour and reputation. Everyone has the right to the protection of the law against such interference or attacks.

ARTICLE 13.   (1) Everyone has the right to freedom of movement and residence within the borders of each state.
(2) Everyone has the right to leave any country, including his own, and to return to his country.

ARTICLE 14.   (1) Everyone has the right to seek and to enjoy in other countries asylum from persecution.
(2) This right may not be invoked in the case of persecutions genuinely arising from nonpolitical crimes or from acts contrary to the purposes and principles of the United Nations.

ARTICLE 15.   (1) Everyone has the right to a nationality.
(2) No one shall be arbitrarily deprived of his nationality nor denied the right to change nationality.

ARTICLE 16.   (1) Men and women of full age, without any limitation due to race, nationality or religion, have the right to marry and found a family. They are entitled to equal rights as to marriage, during marriage and its dissolution.
(2) Marriage shall be entered into only with the free and full consent of the intending spouses.
(3) The family is the natural and fundamental group unit of society and is entitled to protection by society and the State.

ARTICLE 17.   (1) Everyone has the right to own property alone as well as in association with others.
(2) No one shall be arbitrarily deprived of his property.

ARTICLE 18.   Everyone has the right to freedom of thought, conscience and religion; this right includes freedom to change his religion or belief, and freedom, either alone or in community with others and in public or private, to manifest his religion or belief in teaching, practice, worship and observance.

ARTICLE 19. Everyone has the right to freedom of opinion and expression; this right includes the freedom to hold opinions without interference and to seek, receive and impart information and ideas through any media and regardless of frontiers.

ARTICLE 20. (1) Everyone has the right to freedom of peaceful assembly and association.
(2) No one may be compelled to belong to an association.

ARTICLE 21. (1) Everyone has the right to take part in the government of his country, directly or through freely chosen representatives.
(2) Everyone has the right of equal access to public service in his country.
(3) The will of the people shall be the basis of the authority of government; this will shall be expressed in periodic and genuine elections which shall be by universal and equal suffrage and shall be held by secret vote or by equivalent free voting procedure.

ARTICLE 22. Everyone, as a member of society, has the right to social security and is entitled to realization, through national effort and international cooperation, and in accordance with the organization and resources of each State, of the economic, social and cultural rights indispensable for his dignity and the free development of his personality.

ARTICLE 23. (1) Everyone has the right to work, to free choice of employment, to just and favorable conditions of work and to protection against unemployment.
(2) Everyone, without any discrimination, has the right to equal pay for equal work.
(3) Everyone who works has the right to just and favorable remuneration insuring for himself and his family an existence worthy of human dignity, and supplemented, if necessary, by other means of social protection.

(4) Everyone has the right to form and to join trade unions for the protection of his interests.

ARTICLE 24.   Everyone has the right to rest and leisure, including reasonable limitation of working hours and periodic holidays with pay.

ARTICLE 25. (1) Everyone has the right to a standard of living adequate for the health and well-being of himself and of his family, including food, clothing, housing and medical care and necessary social services, and the right to security in the event of unemployment, sickness, disability, widowhood, old age or other lack of livelihood in circumstances beyond control.
(2) Motherhood and childhood are entitled to special care and assistance. All children, whether born in or out of wedlock, shall enjoy the same social protection.

ARTICLE 26. (1) Everyone has the right to education. Education shall be free, at least in the elementary and fundamental stages. Elementary education shall be compulsory. Technical and professional education shall be made generally available and higher education shall be equally accessible to all on the basis of merit.
(2) Education shall be directed to the full development of the human personality and to the strengthening of respect for human rights and fundamental freedoms. It shall promote understanding, tolerance and friendship among all nations, racial or religious groups, and shall further the activities of the United Nations for the maintenance of peace.
(3) Parents have a prior right to choose the kind of education that shall be given to their children.

ARTICLE 27. (1) Everyone has the right freely to participate in the cultural life of the community, to enjoy the arts and to share in scientific advancement and its benefits.
(2) Everyone has the right to the protection of

the moral and material interests resulting from any scientific, literary or artistic production of which he is author.

ARTICLE 28. Everyone is entitled to a social and international order in which the rights and freedoms set forth in this Declaration can be fully realized.

ARTICLE 29. (1) Everyone has duties to the community in which alone the free and full development of his personality is possible.

(2) In the exercise of his rights and freedoms, everyone shall be subject only to such limitations as are determined by law solely for the purpose of securing due recognition and respect for the rights and freedoms of others and of meeting the just requirements of morality, public order and the general welfare in a democratic society.

(3) These rights and freedoms may in no case be exercised contrary to the purposes and principles of the United Nations.

ARTICLE 30. Nothing in this Declaration may be interpreted as implying for any State, group or person any right to engage in any activity or to perform any act aimed at the destruction of any of the rights and freedoms set forth herein.

UNICEF and the world's children

It's Halloween and a time for ringing doorbells. No one is surprised to open the door and find ghosts, goblins and witches standing on the doorstep, paper bags open to receive donations of cookies, candy and apples. "Trick or treat!" they exclaim, holding forth their bags. This ceremony is repeated numerous times by numberless children. But on one particular night at the approach of Halloween, the routine changes. Small masked and costumed boys and girls stand outside the doors of homes all over the United States and Canada, without the customary bags. Instead they carry a little box on which there are the letters spelling UNICEF. "Trick or treat for UNICEF!" they announce. Pennies, nickels, dimes and quarters go into the boxes. In a recent year the sum of $1,750,000 was collected in these little boxes. If you ask the small collectors what the money goes for, they could tell you, "We're collecting for the children of the world who need help. One penny pays for five glasses of milk. A nickel provides enough vaccine to protect five children from tuberculosis. A quarter will pay for enough penicillin to treat and cure six children with yaws."

Another project of UNICEF is the annual sale of Christmas cards that takes place in ninety countries. The designs of the cards are contributed by famous artists of many nationalities. In a recent year a total of 2,800,000 greeting cards were sold. When these cards are purchased and used they are again a reminder of the work that UNICEF is able to do. Fifty children can be protected from tuberculosis from the sale of only one box of cards, and from the sale of five boxes a daily glass of milk can be supplied to forty-two children for one full month.

The name UNICEF is made up of the initials of the original name of a permanent body of the United Nations, the United Nations International Children's Emergency Fund. It had its beginning at a meeting of the United Nations General Assembly on December 11, 1946. The idea for it came out of a suggestion by Fiorello LaGuardia, who was Director-General of the division of the U.N. known as the Economic and Social Council. Mr. LaGuardia proposed that a special fund be started which would help take care of boys and girls who were victims of World War II. The various governments would be asked to contribute to the fund. Contributions would also be accepted from private organizations. The Council voted to accept the plan and it was then placed before the General Assembly and that body voted in favor of it. When the plan was returned to the Economic and Social Council, a board was set up consisting of one member each from twenty-six countries. This was the start of UNICEF. Mr. Maurice Pate was chosen Director and still retains that office.

Now the question before the committee was, how could the young victims of the war best be given immediate help? The answer was obvious. The children were hungry, so the first objective chosen by the board was that of feeding them. To help solve this problem, the nutrition experts of two U.N. committees were consulted. These were FAO (Food and Agriculture Organization) and WHO (World Health Organization). It was immediately necessary to decide what foods would be the most nutritious, the cheapest, the most easily transported, and least likely to spoil before reaching their destination. The greatest need was for milk, so powdered milk was chosen to be sent; also fats, meat and fish, cheese, peas and beans, jam and sugar, cocoa and peanut butter.

It was decided that each of the receiving countries would contribute the same amount of food it was to receive from UNICEF. Also, the countries would be responsible for distributing the food and getting it ready to give to the boys and girls who needed it.

The program was soon put into effect. Feeding centers were set up all over Europe in the countries that had requested help from UNICEF. Soon there were thirty thousand of them. Cups of milk and bowls of soup or stew were handed out to the long lines of children that totaled in the millions. Volunteers from every city, town and village helped. So did the school children. The older boys and girls raised vegetables. The girls cooked food in their cooking classes, all of it going to the feeding centers. They made bright posters to put on the walls, using the magic word UNICEF to show that this was a free feeding station.

But the food wasn't all UNICEF gave to the children. Coats and shoes miraculously appeared at the centers, then medical supplies and soap. From the raw cotton, wool and leather sent by UNICEF, clothing and shoes were made by local workers who were paid by the government. By 1950, a million dollars' worth of hides, leather, wool and cotton had been sent by UNICEF to European countries.

But the need went beyond Europe. In 1948 UNICEF reached out to the countries of the Near and Middle East, to the refugee camps of Palestine, Syria and other countries where children were hungry. And when UNICEF teams visited many countries in Asia, they discovered that there were many millions of boys and girls in need of food and medicines. In the underdeveloped countries of Asia alone there were more than half of the world's 650,000,000 children. To reach these children and those of the economically underdeveloped countries of Europe, Central and South America, and to take care of their future needs, UNICEF realized that a long-range program was the only solution.

The governments of these countries, too, realized that a public health service was sorely needed. They knew that the future of their nations depended upon the future of their children. They requested aid from UNICEF and agreed to match, or more than match, every dollar that was given them. With UNICEF's help and by the support of their own governments, it would be possible to establish hospitals, clinics, health centers and feeding stations to take care of their young people. This long-range program presented a terrific challenge, for not only must good health be maintained by nutritious foods and medicines, but the diseases of children must be wiped out.

The governments of the economically underdeveloped countries were eager to help their children. They consulted the experts from FAO and WHO, and then definite plans were laid before UNICEF with a request for its assistance. With the well-planned programs as set up by the government and the full support of the people in each town or village, UNICEF went to work. Around the world the life-saving programs were set in motion. Food stations were set up and the children were fed. Health centers and clinics were established and children's diseases were fought. Hospitals were maintained to care for the sick and diseased. Training centers were started where doctors and nurses received valuable training to carry on the work that had been started. Manufacturing plants were built to supply the millions of pounds of powdered milk needed by the little ones. The task was endless.

For this long-range program, the emergency character of UNICEF was dropped and in 1953 UNICEF, still retaining the initials for which it was so well known, became simply the United Nations Children's Fund. It was a permanent body of the United Nations, the only one giving direct aid to children. By the end of the following year it had assisted nearly one hundred million children in more than eighty countries. Great strides had been taken in fighting malaria, yaws, tuberculosis and eye diseases, while in many places smallpox, diphtheria and whooping cough had been practically eliminated.

The over-all objectives in every country getting assistance from UNICEF were pretty much the same. They were:

(1) to furnish services for maternal and child health and to establish rural health centers and clinics and training centers for nurses and midwives

(2) to carry out mass health programs against malaria, yaws, tuberculosis, trachoma, leprosy and other diseases

(3) to improve nutrition of children with long-range feeding programs especially with the increased production and use of milk

(4) to give emergency aid in the case of catastrophes such as earthquakes, famine, floods, fire and drought

Workers for UNICEF found that the problems were different in different countries. In Nicaragua, Central America, for instance, UNICEF contributed $100,000 to help build a powdered milk processing plant where dairy farmers took their surplus milk when the yield was high. There it was dried into a powdered product that could be given to the children all year round and not just while fresh milk was plentiful.

In the Philippines, before UNICEF came, ninety per cent of the children of the Islands were undernourished. School feeding programs changed this when UNICEF made it possible for every child to receive one nourishing meal every day.

In South American countries, the worst health menace was malaria. This was also true in Asian countries where three hundred million people were malaria victims every year. Malaria is carried by the female mosquito and the preventive is systematic and continuous spraying of everything in the village with DDT. The spraying program takes three years to be completely successful.

In Indonesia, milk was so scarce that one of UNICEF's first projects was to build a large plant for making a nutritious milk substitute from soya beans, peanuts and malt.

In India, tuberculosis and yaws were the worst menaces to health. UNICEF built powdered milk and penicillin plants there. Cases of yaws, a loathsome disease involving open sores on the skin, incapacitating millions of children, were successfully treated and cured with one shot of penicillin.

In Morocco, UNICEF health centers fought the eye diseases of trachoma and conjunctivitis. In Japan, too, a campaign was carried on against trachoma.

In Korea, the first job was to establish two thousand distribution centers to give two million children a glass of milk daily.

Children around the world who were being helped by UNICEF had a different kind of medicine given to them in the person of Danny Kaye, the comedian. His was the medicine of laughter. As a special "ambassador of goodwill" for UNICEF, Danny Kaye, without payment, entertained the children of more than thirty countries with his singing, dancing and fun. Although seventeen different languages were spoken among these children, none familiar to Danny Kaye, he was able through the common language of joy to commune with them. Wherever he went, he was "the funny man with the red hair." From 1953 to 1958 he traveled 240,000 miles on his goodwill mission. In 1956 he was awarded a medal by *Parents' Magazine* for outstanding service to children during 1955. The following year he was presented with the 1956 Mr. Travel Award by *Travel Magazine*. One of the qualifications for this award was "to help further the cause of world peace and mutual understanding among nations and individuals as a result of his travels." One of the results of his work with the world's children was a television film, "The Secret Life of Danny Kaye." It was filmed over a period of three and one half years while he was traveling a distance of one hundred thousand miles for UNICEF. By arrangement with the United Nations, the film was shown simultaneously in twenty-five countries. Its purpose was to let the people of the world know what UNICEF was doing. As an illustration of what the organization meant to the individual child, Danny Kaye has told of a small boy who held up his cup to receive milk, saying, "UNICEF, please," because he thought the word for milk was "UNICEF."

And so the work of UNICEF went on throughout the world. In a recent year UNICEF aided fifty-five million mothers and children with its life-saving programs. For every dollar given by the Fund, governments of the assisted countries "matched" it with from $2 to $2.50. With its steadily increasing ability to bring good health and well-being to the world's children, what would the future hold for UNICEF?

Maurice Pate, Director of the Children's Fund, sums up future projects as an opportunity to expand agricultural programs in economically underdeveloped countries. Also "to encourage the supplementary production of larger amounts of protective foods for local consumption by the village and farm people themselves; to training of workers in agricultural extension; to building the basic framework of permanent health services . . . building up a strong health staff at district or provincial level." And he added as a further objective: to attempt to educate the child "to be a constructive producing citizen of the community."

With these future goals in mind, the role of UNICEF will be to continue to bring aid where it is most needed. By its wonderful work of assistance, it can make healthy bodies to help build healthy minds for the world's future citizens. Surely this is a great contribution toward the brotherhood of the world.

part VI

PROMOTING PEACE AND
UNDERSTANDING

PROMOTING PEACE AND UNDERSTANDING

*The vocation of every man and woman
is to serve other people.*

—TOLSTOY

We have seen how the nations of the world are striving for peace within the framework of the United Nations. Countless individuals in many countries are working tirelessly toward the same goal, and most of them have sacrificed personal careers to devote themselves to the common aim. Many will remain unknown to the general public, but the names of some are recognized throughout the world. Included here are biographies of four whose contributions to brotherhood through the United Nations have been outstanding: Dag Hammarskjold, Ralph Bunche, Eleanor Roosevelt and Marian Anderson. Mahatma Gandhi, whose life was dedicated to attaining equality for all men through peaceful methods, belongs in this section too. And, finally, we have included Alfred Nobel, whose name has become synonymous with man's efforts toward peace.

Dag Hammarskjold:
symbol of the United Nations

When Dag Hammarskjold was killed in an airplane crash over Africa on September 18, 1961, his name was probably the best known in the world. When he first was elected Secretary-General of the United Nations on April 7, 1953, his name was little known outside his native Sweden. Even there, although he held a high governmental office, he was not always recognized.

The story has been told that at the time he was Chairman of the Board of the National Bank of Sweden, he still enjoyed going on bicycle trips through the countryside by himself for relaxation. One evening, hatless and wearing his customary shorts and sport shirt, he stopped at a hotel and asked for a room for the night. The desk clerk, glancing at the youthful-looking man in casual attire, directed him to a youth hostel down the street. And Hammarskjold, accepting the clerk's suggestion without causing him any embarrassment, took his advice and stayed that night at the hostel. This incident, trivial as it seems, is typical of Dag Hammarskjold's modesty.

Dag Hammarskjold, christened Dag Hjalmar Agne Carl Hammarskjold, was born in Jonkoping, Sweden, on July 29, 1905. He was the youngest of the four sons of Kurt Hjalmar Leonard and Agnes (Almquist) Hammarskjold. His father, a stern, rather forbidding person, had long been in Swedish politics. During World War I, he was Prime Minister of Sweden and had been instrumental in keeping that country neutral.

His mother was a different type of personality. Although she, too, was brilliant, she was warm and friendly and had an ability to get along well with other people, a trait her son Dag inherited.

143

But even as a child, although he was well liked by his schoolmates and got along well with them, Dag was not the sort of person who had close and intimate friends. This may have been because he had the reputation of being the smartest student in the class and the rest of the boys stood a little in awe of him. This same feeling on the part of his fellow students continued through his university days as well. He attended Uppsala University and, as it was in the same city where his parents resided, he lived at home and so missed the intimate friendships formed through living with other students.

During the vacation days he loved to hike or bicycle through the Swedish countryside. He never lost his liking for this type of recreation and believed that one had to be able to feel the earth and the sky in order to hear clearly one's own thoughts.

From the very beginning, Dag Hammarskjold's ambition was to be in governmental service and he never had an inclination to enter any other profession. He believed that the government had a great need for men who were dedicated to working for it, and for this reason he never formally joined any political party. He preferred to describe himself as an independent. He felt that in giving service to one's country one had to sacrifice all personal feelings too, and that was the reason he never married. He said that he could never ask a woman to share a life with one whose work was his first consideration.

In 1945, Mr. Hammarskjold was appointed financial and economic adviser to the Swedish Cabinet. Two years later he was named Under-Secretary to the Foreign Ministry. In 1951, he was one of the Swedish delegates to the United Nations meeting in Paris and the next year acted as the delegation's chairman when the U.N. met in New York.

Early in 1953, it was apparent that the United Nations was going to have to elect a new Secretary-General. Trygve Lie, who had been in office, was no longer acceptable to the Soviet Union, which had opposed the U.N.'s action during the war in Korea. It was understood that a compromise candidate would have to be chosen and Hammarskjold was proposed by the French delegation. The suggestion was a complete surprise to just about everyone, and even our own State Department knew very little about him; but it was soon learned that Hammarskjold was considered by his colleagues to be a brilliant administrator although he worked in a quiet way.

If the suggestion of Hammarskjold came as a surprise to the U.N. delegations, it was nothing compared with the way Hammarskjold himself felt when he heard about it. He was in Sweden at the time and at first didn't believe the newspaper reports. But when he got official word from the Security Council he had to make his decision. On April 9, 1953, he arrived in New York and on the next day, before the delegates from sixty nations, took the oath of office.

"I, Dag Hammarskjold, solemnly swear to exercise in all loyalty, discretion and conscience the functions entrusted to me as Secretary-General of the United Nations, to discharge these functions and regulate my conduct with the interests of the United Nations only in view and not to seek or accept instructions in regard to the performance of my duties from any government or other authority external to the government."

This solemn oath of office Dag Hammarskjold considered sacred, and he never wavered from carrying it out to the best of his ability. Indeed, after his fatal air crash, it was found that he was carrying a copy of it in a book he had taken with him on his trip.

Reporters who covered the U.N. when Dag Hammarskjold was elected Secretary-General thought they were going to have trouble pronouncing his name. But he assured them it was really very simple. "Hammer-shuld" was correct or if they preferred they could say "Hammer-shield."

Hammarskjold believed that the Secretary-General's office should be run in a systematic way with as few people as possible. He thought that a small staff could accomplish more working together in an intimate way than a large one. The idea worked—and so did his staff. It was nothing for the Secretary-General to work half the night, and sometimes his undersecretaries Andrew Cordier and Ralph Bunche would sit up until three or four o'clock in the morning discussing with him the latest world crisis.

As time went on Hammarskjold came to personify the U.N. to many people. If a knotty problem came up, delegates would say, "Let Dag do it." And usually Dag did! He had great faith in the U.N. as a place where men could share a common hope. He believed firmly that most people have a desire for decency and that they realize that this same desire exists in other people as well as themselves. Therefore if the U.N. comes to be a symbol of that desire no one will ever want to tear it down.

He felt, too, that the U.N. was the organization to which the small and the middle powers could turn for support. Sometimes the smaller countries didn't want aid from the larger ones for fear of coming too much under their domination. But the U.N. was prepared to help them and Hammarskjold helped to foster this idea among them. Another characteristic of the man which helped to inspire confidence in him as Secretary-General was his insistence on treating every conference with him in the strictest confidence. He never forgot for one minute that what was said to him in private was always to remain that way.

Dag Hammarskjold, at the time of his death, was fifty-six years old but he looked much younger. He was of medium height and had blond hair and blue eyes. He seemed relaxed but always a little aloof, and while friendly with his associates, had very few close friends. He was very intellectual. He enjoyed music, poetry and art. He liked the theater, too, but the pressing business of U.N. affairs kept him from attending very often. He maintained an attractive apartment in New York City where he occasionally gave small diplomatic or private parties. He was not interested in attending many social functions unless they were of a diplomatic nature. For relaxation, he had a small estate near Brewster, New York, where he could spend the weekend hiking and enjoying nature.

He wrote all his own speeches and they were effective but never very colorful. He avoided using expressions just for their effect. He believed the delegates would lose confidence in a Secretary-General who strove to be dramatic. He always tried to avoid the spotlight.

One of his beliefs, that men need to be alone sometimes, was brought into focus when one of his pet projects came into being. This was the Meditation Room at the U.N.—in his own words a "room of stillness" where one could be quiet and at peace.

During the time Dag Hammarskjold was Secretary-General of the United Nations he found that one of his hardest jobs in the administrative line was the assigning of jobs. First of all he demanded that those filling the jobs must be not only fully qualified for the work they were to do but that they must have integrity and be impartial and independent. This meant that they must be prepared to put consideration for the U.N. ahead of that for their own countries. Not only was it hard to find men who qualified but also there was the problem of choosing too many from any one country lest the delegates from another country become jealous.

In his years in office Hammarskjold was to have both successes and failures in his attempts to deal fairly with countries and to solve crises which demanded his intervention.

One of the first problems Hammarskjold found waiting for him in 1953, on assuming the Secretary-General's office, was the matter of the American airmen shot down during the Korean War and still held prisoners by the Chinese Communists. Hammarskjold was always a believer in personal diplomacy, so he decided to go to Peiping and have a conference with Premier Chou En-lai. Although his visit turned out in the end to have favorable results, these were not known until about six months later. Chou En-lai was very careful not to have it seem that he was yielding to U.N. pressure because that would make him "lose face" with his own people as well as the rest of the world. Rather, he waited until Hammarskjold's birthday before he released the flyers and then he made it seem a personal gesture of friendship to the Secretary-General rather than a matter of living up to the terms of a former agreement.

For years a trouble spot in the world had been the Middle East. In 1956, the situation had developed to such a point that if Hammarskjold and the U.N. had not acted swiftly it might have exploded into World War III. The trouble was between Israel and Egypt and more than once Hammarskjold flew over to confer with the leaders of the two countries—Nasser of Egypt and Ben Gurion of Israel. In July, 1956, Nasser of Egypt announced he was taking over the Suez Canal which had been under British control through an agreement with Egypt. This agreement was to expire in 1968. Nasser gave as his reason that he needed the money he would collect from ships passing through the canal to build a dam Egypt needed. Border troubles between Israel and Egypt which had always been bad became worse and Israel invaded the Sinai Peninsula. The Sinai Peninsula extends along the east side of the Suez Canal between the Gulf of Suez and the Gulf of 'Aqaba. Israel claimed that Egypt, which owned the Peninsula, had military bases there and was bombing Israel from them.

The United States delegates to the U.N., along with other U.N. diplomats, were even more stunned at the turn of events when they learned that Israel's move had the backing of France and Britain. Egypt rejected a cease-fire on Israel which was demanded by France and Britain, and on October 31 Britain and France bombed Egypt by

air. Early in November France and Britain landed forces to compel
Egypt to give up the Suez Canal.

In the meantime, the U.N. under Hammarskjold was working frantically to arrange a cease-fire and on November 7 finally succeeded.
The fighting stopped, the U.N. formed the first international police
force to supervise the truce in the Middle East, and soldiers from neutral countries were sent in. The U.N. also took over the task of removing the bombed vessels which were blocking the Suez Canal. Under
the cease-fire agreement, Egypt was to keep control of the canal and
agreed to spend a certain amount of the revenue she received to maintain repairs. But no agreement was able to be made which would permit Israel to use the canal. However, U.N. intervention had saved the
world at that point from a truly great tragedy.

But while the Suez crisis was at its height, another trouble just as
tragic was brewing. Hungary, controlled since World War II by Russia, revolted against her Soviet-dominated government. Soviet forces
moved swiftly in and crushed the uprising completely. Hammarskjold
wanted to send in U.N. observers to see what was happening but was
refused permission by Hungarian and Soviet officials. No other nation
except one or two small ones was prepared to do more about it than
to bring moral pressure. Because of the timing of the Budapest insur-
rection and the Suez crisis, it was never even suggested in the U.N.
that Hammarskjold go to Budapest personally. At that time he did
not feel he could go without authorization from either the Security
Council or the General Assembly of the U.N. This was one of the
times when the U.N. was ineffective in trying to stop a wrong from
being committed.

When Hammarskjold took office in the U.N. in 1953, four African
nations were among the members. By the end of 1960, there were
twenty-six. Some of these small African nations had, with some aid,
managed the change-over from a Colonial possession to an independent government successfully and were well started. But conditions
in the Congo went from bad to worse and a very confusing situation
developed.

Belgium had owned the Congo for many years and had just recently withdrawn. The change had come so suddenly that the Congolese were not prepared with skilled and trained men to take over.
Event after event happened so rapidly that no one was ever sure what
the next day would bring forth. The Congolese army, still com-

manded by Belgian officers, revolted against them and Katanga province, the richest in the Congo, announced it was seceding and was establishing itself as a separate state. The Congolese leaders wanted the U.N. to use force to keep Katanga from doing this. The U.N. had already given the Congo technical aid and had even sent in a U.N. force to restore order when the army revolted. But it did not believe in interfering with the internal problems of a country. So Lumumba, the Congo's Prime Minister, appealed to Russia and did everything he could to harass the U.N. personnel stationed in the Congo.

When Russian aid was given directly to the Congo instead of through the U.N. the matter was taken up before the Security Council. A few days later a new Congolese leader displaced Lumumba and ordered the whole Soviet program of "aid" to the Congo to cease.

Through all this turmoil of changing leaders in the Congo, accusations by the Russians that Hammarskjold was favoring Belgium, charges by Belgium that the U.N. operation in the Congo was a failure, and even doubt by other nations that the U.N. was acting effectively, the Secretary-General tried to keep calm. He wanted only the welfare of the Congo and believed the situation could eventually be settled by persuasion and not by force.

But the Soviets blamed Hammarskjold for their failure to get a foothold in the Congo and were determined to wreck him if they could. With this purpose in mind Chairman Khrushchev came to the U.N. and in an impassioned speech demanded the resignation of Hammarskjold. Indeed, he wanted the office of Secretary-General to be changed to what he called a "troika." This would be a three-man office made up of representatives from the West, the East and a neutral nation.

Hammarskjold realized, as did everyone else, that this would mean the death of the United Nations. All decisions would be stalemated and the U.N. would finally cease to function. At the next U.N. meeting after Khrushchev's speech, Hammarskjold answered him. With the utmost dignity and courage he announced that he would not resign but would remain at his post so long as the other nations wished him to do so. While Khrushchev sat and thumped his desk to show his disapproval, the other delegates, with the exception of the Soviet block, rose and gave Hammarskjold a standing ovation. It was one of the most moving scenes the United Nations had ever witnessed.

In September, 1961, Dag Hammarskjold decided once again to

visit the African leaders in the Congo and the Katanga province in an effort to bring unity and peace to that troubled country. On Monday, September 18, it was reported in the early morning news that his plane, due to land at Ndola in northern Rhodesia, was overdue. Those who heard that early morning broadcast were shocked and disbelieving. But as the morning wore on it became more and more evident that it was true that something had happened to his plane. Later in the day its wreckage was found just four miles from Ndola where it had been scheduled to land the night before.

Dag Hammarskjold was dead and the whole world had lost a friend.

In October, 1961, it was announced that the 1961 Nobel Peace Prize had been awarded to Dag Hammarskjold. It was the first time in the history of the award that it had been bestowed on a person no longer living. Some weeks later, the beautiful U.N. library was dedicated to this man of peace.

When Dag Hammarskjold made his first speech as Secretary-General of the United Nations, he ended with words quoted from a Swedish poet—words that could just as well have been his own, so firmly did he believe them.

> "The greatest prayer of man is not
> for victory but for peace."

Ralph J. Bunche: champion for peace

The handsome, distinguished-looking gentleman at the head table was addressing an assembly of a thousand persons who had gathered at the Waldorf-Astoria in New York on July 1, 1949, to do him honor. He concluded his speech with words that went straight to the heart of his listeners, for they knew that they expressed so well what the speaker himself stood for.

"I have a number of very strong biases," he told them in his clear voice. "I have a deep-seated bias against hate and intolerance. I have a bias against racial and religious bigotry. I have a bias against war, and a bias for peace. I have a bias which leads me to believe in the essential goodness of my fellow men, which leads me to believe that no problem of human relations is ever insoluble. I have a strong bias in favor of the United Nations and its ability to maintain a peaceful world."

This man whose genius was being honored by such a large audience of distinguished citizens was Dr. Ralph J. Bunche, a world-famous American diplomat who had received more honorary degrees than any other person in the United States and had been awarded the Nobel Prize for Peace. One of the greatest citizens America has ever produced, Ralph Bunche has traveled a long way since his humble beginnings in the shabby little house on Orleans Street in the Negro district of Detroit.

Grandson of a slave, he was born over his father's barber shop in Detroit on August 7, 1904. Money was scarce in the household which consisted of his parents, his grandmother and two aunts and, later, a little sister. And so while he was still a small boy he became a wage-earner by running errands and selling papers on the street. When he realized that the Negroes in his district had few pennies to spend on newspapers, he began venturing into the world of the whites where he found it much easier to dispose of his wares.

When he was eleven years old the family moved to the Southwest because of his parents' poor health. On the train trip from Detroit to Albuquerque Ralph discovered for the first time that Negroes were segregated in what were called Jim Crow cars. This was his first real awareness that he had been born into a divided world of whites and blacks. But he was excited to be traveling through so much of the United States and thrilled, when they reached New Mexico, to see his first Indian.

Only a few months after they arrived in Albuquerque Ralph's mother died and three months later his father was dead, leaving Ralph and his little sister, Grace, orphans. But they had Grandma Johnson. Grandma Johnson was a thin little woman less than five feet tall, wiry and strong of will. She determined that, come what may, Ralph was to receive an education. For as long as he could remember and on through his boyhood until her death after he had graduated from college, "Nana" was always there, directing and scolding, advising and loving, smoothing the way and giving courage when things looked dark. He could remember how, when he was a very small boy, she had taken him on her lap and told him, "Remember, it's not the color of your skin that matters. It's what's in your heart and in your head." Grandma Johnson determined that Ralph must have the opportunity to put lots of things in his head. She directed their whole lives toward getting Ralph educated.

The family finally settled in Los Angeles, where Ralph graduated as an honor student from elementary school when he was fourteen. As an errand boy for the *Los Angeles Times* that summer he was able to earn eight dollars a week. The family was so poor that it must have been a temptation for Ralph to quit school and keep his job, but Grandma would have none of it. He entered Jefferson High School, where he was one of a very few Negro pupils. Here he always had outside jobs, but because of his remarkable vitality he also took part in many extracurricular activities. He became a member of the debating team and played basketball, football and baseball. When he was graduated in 1922 he was among the ten top students and won medals in several of his studies. And his participation in athletics gave him the opportunity to go to college. He was offered a four-year scholarship to the University of California in Los Angeles. As much as this meant to the boy, he felt that his earnings, small though they might be, were sorely needed by his family. But Grandma made the decision for him: he was to go, of course!

Ralph Bunche has never been afraid of hard work. His tenacity in sticking with a job until it was finished, and his determination to give it all he had, not only helped him to get a fine education but proved invaluable to him in his career later as a political scientist and as a successful diplomat. His four years at U.C.L.A. took hard work and perseverence. He started his freshman year there by leaving the house at five every morning to fill his role of janitor of the women's gymnasium, scrubbing floors and washing windows, grabbing a cup of coffee and making it to nine o'clock classes. After a few months he became seriously ill and had to undergo an operation. His convalescence was so slow that he couldn't return to school at all that year. But the following September he again entered the freshman class and went on working and studying. Besides continuing with his janitor's job he worked during his lunch hour in the cafeteria. But somehow he stayed with the top of his class, winning membership in the Phi Beta Kappa society for his scholarship, and besides found time to play basketball, be sports editor of the yearbook and take an active part on the debating team. When Grandma Johnson, his aunts and his sister attended his college graduation they thrilled with pride to see him receive five medals and graduate *summa cum laude*. But the thing that made "Nana" proudest of all was the fellowship he won for graduate work at Harvard University! To Ralph, the obstacles for accepting this offer must have seemed staggering. But again Grandma was all for it. She was certain now that her brilliant grandson was destined for big things in this world. With her usual faith she was sure there would be a way. And her faith was rewarded when a group in Los Angeles donated a thousand dollars to send Ralph east to Harvard.

It was almost as though his tiny, frail grandmother, with her determination and unquenchable spirit, had lived only for such valid proof of her boy's future, for shortly after his graduation she died suddenly. Her death was a great blow to him, for she had been his acknowledged strength during all the early part of his life.

The serious young student who started classes in the graduate school at Harvard was immensely impressed with the university, its faculty and its traditions. But because his financial problem was always present, he had had to find quarters in the Negro section of Boston. Here he became more and more aware of the squalor in which most Negroes were forced to live, and of the color line that was so apparent in the housing situation in this and most other cities in the United States. As a small boy in Detroit he might have been aware of segregation. But on his journey in a Jim Crow car through the Southern states he must have seen that he was being treated differently from the white people. Later, as he grew up in Los Angeles, it was apparent that few Negroes were able to afford an education, and that a lack of it kept them from rising to a place of economic security in the world. Now at Harvard, as he formed new friendships with other Negro students, this subject was often discussed. These graduate students were thinking men, many of whom became prominent in their fields later on. All of them were disturbed and thoughtful over the great problems that American Negroes were facing. They often talked long into the night and Ralph Bunche, as a political science student, impressed the others with his valid arguments on this and other subjects.

In 1928 he won his master's degree in political science from Harvard and was immediately offered several positions in universities, but the one he accepted was with Howard, the famous Negro university in Washington, D.C. Again, he found that he had to live in a segregated part of the city.

He set up a new political science department at Howard and one of his pupils was an attractive young woman named Ruth Harris who was studying to become a teacher. Mutual interests and admiration for each other soon deepened into love and Ralph and Ruth became engaged. They agreed to wait to be married so that Ralph could obtain his doctorate, and that goal soon became visible when he was given another fellowship at Harvard. He taught and studied there for a year and in June, 1930, he and Ruth were married. While he was again teaching at Howard University he received a Julius Rosenwald Fellowship, which gave him an opportunity to travel abroad and collect material for his thesis. First he went to England and Europe, then to Africa for a three-months tour, which included a month interviewing African tribesmen in small villages.

In 1934 he was awarded his Ph.D. in political science from Harvard, and in 1936 he continued his studies, while on leave from Howard University, by taking courses at Northwestern University, the London School of Economics and the University of Capetown in South Africa. Even Grandma Johnson would have been amazed at the extent of her grandson's education. He kept his teaching post as head of his department at Howard. He was now a man well respected in the teaching world, a recognized scholar. But it had not been easy for him and his wife and two little girls to live in Washington where racial segregation was, as he has said, the worst of any city he had ever known. As time went on he spent more and more time studying the racial problem. His writings on the subject were printed in national magazines. He was away from home often now, traveling all over the United States, Europe, Africa and the East Indies on special studies in race relationships. He had accepted a position as co-director of the Institute of Race Relations at Swarthmore College. Then in 1938 he took part in a most extensive study of the Negro in America conducted by a Swedish sociologist, Gunnar Myrdal. For this project Dr. Bunche prepared over three thousand pages of detailed reports. This experience in writing up reports from facts stood him in good stead in his later work.

Because of his knowledge of African affairs he was made head of the African research department in the Office of Strategic Services for the U.S. Government. Then came the offer from Secretary of State Hull for him to take over a position in the State Department in the Territorial Studies Division. Ralph Bunche was the first Negro ever to serve in the State Department. He had been chosen over other men as the most capable and experienced man available.

Ralph Bunche was on his way to a service that was to benefit not only his own country but the entire world, for his next assignment was to attend the Dumbarton Oaks Conference in Washington in August, 1944. He also attended the San Francisco Conference as adviser to the United States delegate, and helped to form the United Nations Charter.

Dr. Bunche was given the opportunity to serve the United Nations in a more active way in 1947, when he was asked by the Secretary-General of the U.N., Trygve Lie, to see what could be done to maintain peace between the Arabs and the Jews in Palestine. Members of the U.N. knew that the explosive situation might break into a serious war at any moment, and one of the most vital reasons for the establishment of the United Nations was to settle disputes between nations by arbitration. To prove itself effective the U.N. had to end the fighting in Palestine, so Count Folke Bernadotte was appointed as official mediator between the two warring nations. Dr. Bunche, who had already spent eight months in Palestine for the U.N., was told to instruct Bernadotte in what had been done up to this point. After Count Bernadotte had received Dr. Bunche's two-hundred-page detailed report he cabled congratulations to the U.N. on the man they had given to aid him in his work as mediator.

Months of negotiations went on, all unsuccessful. In traveling about, the lives of the U.N. representatives were endangered many times by fanatics who resented their presence in the country. On September 17, 1948, Count Bernadotte and a French officer who had been mistaken for Bunche were killed by gunfire as their car drew up before the U.N. headquarters in Jerusalem. The Secretary-General immediately asked Dr. Bunche to take over in Bernadotte's place.

This was the hardest assignment Ralph Bunche had ever been given.

When he accepted it his heart was heavy over the loss of his friend and filled with doubts over his mission, because at that time the state of affairs in Palestine appeared almost hopeless.

His final success in ending the war in Palestine is an exciting story. It was no wonder that the problem was considered almost insoluble, with the Jews on the one hand determined to remain in their new state of Israel and the Arabs on the other hand adamant about their rights to the land where they had lived for thousands of years. But Ralph Bunche told them, "This war must be stopped," and he had the Jewish and Arab representatives come to the neutral Island of Rhodes where the U.N. negotiations were taking place. He had them meet time and time again—in short meetings that often ended with quick tempers and frustrations, and long meetings that often lasted far into the night. Ralph Bunche worked incessantly, day and night, with little food and rest. The meetings went on for weeks and then for months, a situation Dr. Bunche had foreseen, for when they began he had remarked, "I'll never adjourn this meeting. I'll stay for ten years if necessary."

Finally, in January, 1949, at a meeting that lasted twenty hours, Egypt and Israel signed a cease-fire truce. It was a golden moment for Bunche, one that he had worked for with every ounce of tact, patience, perseverance and persuasiveness that he possessed. As he signed the document for the United Nations he must have felt a personal triumph along with his rejoicing for what this would mean to the United Nations and the world.

The ending of the war meant that the United Nations had accomplished what it had been incorporated to do when it was formed back in San Francisco—to settle by negotiation rather than by bloodshed the differences between nations. Telegrams of congratulation came to Ralph Bunche and when he returned to New York he was received by a typical New York ticker-tape parade. Then he was asked to go on a speaking tour to tell the people of the United States about the United Nations.

It seemed as though everyone wanted to hear him speak. He accepted as many invitations as possible, talking about the work of the U.N. as an instrument of peace. Wherever he went he was honored. Aside from numerous honorary degrees conferred upon him by universities, he was presented with medals, plaques and scrolls by cities across the nation. The United States Government honored him by offering him the position of Assistant Secretary of State. Dr. Bunche turned down this post, and as usual he was honest in his reason for doing so. He told President Truman that he could not subject his family to the racial discrimination in the Capital city. And he told the newsmen when they interviewed him, "I once served my time there. Now I want to live as a free man."

In a Commencement address at a Negro college in the South, Dr. Bunche spoke of the problems ahead for the graduates and reminded them that their paths, as Negroes, would not be easy. "Though the Negro has made and is making great progress," he said, "very much remains to be done . . . The rate of progress will depend in large degree upon the preparation and ability, the determination and the courage of these young Negroes. They must never relax in the struggle for full citizenship for the Negro, for the complete integration of American Negroes in the life of the Nation. They must be ever alert."

He said further: "I am reasonably optimistic about the future of race relations in America. The conscience of the Nation quickens. An ever-increasing number of citizens, South as well as North, realize that our bad race relations are immensely damaging to the Nation, and they are determined to do something about it. The forces of true democracy are strongly at work in our society and the force of democracy on the march is irresistible."

One of the greatest honors that can be bestowed upon a man came to Ralph Bunche when in 1950 he was awarded the Nobel Prize for Peace.

He had worked for and with the United Nations in some capacity since its inception. Since 1958, as Under-Secretary of Special Political Affairs for the United Nations, he has been the highest-ranking U.S. citizen in the U.N. Secretariat. He has never ceased to work for peace. In a speech delivered at the Western College Conference on United Nations Affairs held at Stanford University, he talked about the importance of freedom as a requisite of world peace.

"Peace in the world can be secure only where there is universal human freedom," he said, "when men as individuals are free to go and come; to speak, think, worship, assemble and associate freely; to earn their daily bread, and enough of it, by voluntary labor; to feel secure and without fear in their daily lives; when every man, whatever his race or color or creed, whatever his culture or origin, can walk with full dignity and on a plane of equality with all other men. Certainly, for all peoples who have enjoyed freedom, peace and freedom are inseparable."

With the same determination that he showed when he sold papers on the street as a small boy, Ralph Johnson Bunche is selling the United Nations today to all who will listen. He believes it will save the world from destructive wars; he believes that it will build a constructive world for peoples everywhere.

Eleanor Roosevelt:
advocate of human rights

"Mrs. Roosevelt," he said in his rather deep voice, "we would like to know if you would serve on Committee 3."

The deep voice belonged to Senator Arthur H. Vandenburg, a member of the United States delegation sent to London in 1946 to help organize the United Nations. Mrs. Roosevelt, asked by President Truman to be a member of the same delegation, was on board the *Queen Elizabeth* bound for London when Senator Vandenburg made this request.

At the time she was asked to serve on it she didn't even know what Committee 3 was going to have to do. But as Eleanor Roosevelt had been brought up to believe that you do what you ought to do, not what you want to, she accepted. She only knew that whatever work was involved, she would try to the best of her ability to accomplish what was requested of her.

Eleanor Roosevelt was born on October 11, 1884. She was the oldest of three children, a girl and two boys, born to Elliott and Anna Hall Roosevelt. Eleanor was a shy little girl who craved affection. She received much from her father and completely adored him, but she always stood a little in awe of her beautiful mother, although she admired her intensely. Somehow she always felt that her mother was disappointed because she wasn't beautiful. And when her mother called her "Granny" because of her serious expression it only increased her shyness. Indeed, she was so shy that even in the small private class she attended she found it hard to spell orally the simple words she knew perfectly.

With her father she felt completely at ease. Elliott Roosevelt was devoted to her too, and allowed his young daughter to accompany him whenever it was possible. One time, he took her with him to the newsboys' clubhouse to help serve their Thanksgiving dinner. Young as she was, she somehow realized that there were children who were unfortunate and didn't have as much as she. She never forgot that day.

Her father's praise was very important to her and one of her early desires was to be a great singer because she knew how much he admired singers. She was always trying to please her family and would do anything to win their approval.

Unfortunately her father was not well. He had had a number of early illnesses and, later on, a serious riding accident. The result was that he was obliged to spend much of his time away from home in an attempt to recover his health. During these periods the children and their mother spent their summers at Grandmother Hall's summer home at Tivoli, New York. Their winter home was in New York City.

Then more unhappiness came. Eleanor's mother became ill with diphtheria and died. She had made her mother guardian of her three children, and so it was arranged that they would live with their grandmother. Although Elliott Roosevelt adored his children it was understood that he was unable to have them with him.

The same winter of Eleanor's mother's death, her little brother Elliott, Jr., died too. And the summer before she was ten years old, word was received of the death of her father. Although she grieved deeply, there was something inside her that made her refuse to accept the fact that she would never see her adored father again. Somehow it seemed to her that he was closer to her than ever.

Grandmother Hall had always left the disciplining of her own children to her husband. But now she was resolved to be stricter with her grandchildren. As a result the word "no" was heard more often than "yes." Sundays were strictly observed. No games were played and only special books could be read. But there was one pleasure. On Sunday evenings the whole family would gather around the piano. While Eleanor's Aunt Pussie played hymns, the rest joined in singing. Eleanor always remembered what happy times these were.

Grandmother Hall and Eleanor's aunts had one idea that caused Eleanor a great deal of discomfort. They believed in dressing her in a fashion which they thought made her look younger. Now Eleanor was tall for her age and it made her self-conscious to go to parties in dresses above her knees when the other girls, in accordance with the style, wore them much longer. And how uncomfortable were the long black stockings and the high button shoes that she wore both summer and winter!

While her father was alive she visited her Roosevelt relatives occasionally. But with his death, visits with them became fewer. However she was allowed one or two summer visits with her Aunt Edith and Uncle Ted at their Sagamore Hill home at Oyster Bay, New York, and her grandmother also permitted her to visit them during the Christmas holidays. It was at one of the parties given for their young people that Eleanor first danced with a distant cousin named Franklin Delano Roosevelt, who lived at Hyde Park, New York.

When Eleanor was a little girl she had attended private classes rather than public school. The year she was fifteen, her grandmother decided to send her to a girls' boarding school in England. The one chosen was Mlle. Sovestre's "Allenswood," just outside of London. The next three years were spent abroad—winters in school and summers traveling in Europe.

The winter after she came home her name was placed on the debutante list and she received invitations to many parties. Because she had been away for so long she had lost touch with many of her old friends and she was still shy. Her first dance was pure agony and she was sure she was a social failure. Later on, as she resumed old friendships, she enjoyed parties more, and she wouldn't have missed going to them for anything, as she had been brought up to believe that "Society" was very important.

That year was a real milestone in her life. She began to see more and more of her cousin, Franklin Roosevelt, who at that time was attending Harvard. He graduated in June, 1904, and the next autumn their engagement was announced.

The wedding took place on March 17, 1905, at the home of a cousin in New York City. Her Uncle Theodore, at that time President of the United States, gave her away.

There was a St. Patrick's Day parade in New York the day of her marriage and between the persons gathered to watch the parade and those who wanted a glimpse of the President, the crowd on the streets became so large that some of the invited guests couldn't get through and didn't arrive at the wedding until after the ceremony.

The young Roosevelts' first years of married life were spent in New York City where Franklin was a member of a law firm. Then in 1910 he decided to run for the state legislature and was elected. This election meant a great change in the life of his wife. It meant moving to Albany, where for the first time in her life Eleanor would be completely independent. Up until this time her mother-in-law had always been within call for advice, but now she was on her own. Besides managing her home she had three young children to care for, Anna Eleanor, James and Elliott. Another child, the first Franklin, Jr., had died in infancy.

Although she had a nurse for her children she tried to spend as much time as possible with them herself, and besides her duties as homemaker and mother she found herself becoming more and more involved in her husband's public life. At first an interest in politics seemed to be her duty as a wife, but soon her interest grew real as she began to learn that in the field of government service one meets all kinds of people whose ideas add to one's own education.

In 1912, Franklin Roosevelt was re-elected to the New York State Senate. At the time of the campaign he was ill with typhoid fever and turned its management over to Louis Howe, a newspaper man. From that time on Louis Howe became one of Franklin Roosevelt's most devoted admirers and believed from the beginning that he was destined to be great.

Early in 1913 when the newly elected President, Woodrow Wilson, was choosing his cabinet, he appointed Franklin Roosevelt as Assistant Secretary of the Navy. Roosevelt promptly resigned from the New York Senate and moved his family to Washington.

If Eleanor Roosevelt had thought her life was a busy one while she was living in Albany, it was nothing compared with her life in Washington. There were social calls that had to be made. That first year a part of each day was devoted to them, beginning on Monday with the wives of the Supreme Court Justices and ending on Friday with the wives of the diplomats. In between were calls on the wives of Congressmen, Cabinet members and Senators. In August of that year another son, Franklin Jr., was born.

During President Wilson's first term of office, war broke out in Europe. One result of this was that many European diplomats came to Washington, each one trying to get the most from the United States for his country, and social life became more hectic than ever. To make it even more complicated for Mrs. Roosevelt, there was a new baby in the Roosevelt home whom they named John.

And now the war clouds were growing darker and eventually the United States was drawn into what became known in later years as World War I. Eleanor Roosevelt, although hating war intensely, was anxious to do what she could and offered her services to the Red Cross canteen. When there was a particularly deadly influenza epidemic raging in 1918, she took care of her husband and five children, who were stricken. In addition to this she kept on with her Red Cross duties and also helped to care for girls working in Washington who were ill and far away from their homes.

The end of World War I brought new experiences. Franklin Roosevelt was chosen to go to Paris to take care of some Navy affairs. Mrs. Roosevelt went with him and learned firsthand what it meant to see a country that had been devastated by war.

The year 1920 saw a new Presidential campaign and again Mrs. Roosevelt became interested in politics. Franklin Roosevelt was nominated for Vice President on the Democratic ticket as the running mate of James Cox. They were defeated by Warren G. Harding and Calvin Coolidge.

And then came the never-to-be-forgotten summer of 1921. The Roosevelt family was in the habit of spending its summers at Campobello Island, New Brunswick, Canada. That summer, tragedy came. Franklin Roosevelt was stricken with polio and for a time it seemed as though his government career was over. But although his legs remained paralyzed, his spirit did not. Encouraged by his wife, Louis Howe and Governor Alfred E. Smith of New York, he became active once more in the political field. In 1928, the same year Governor Smith ran for President, Franklin D. Roosevelt was elected Governor of New York State.

At her husband's request, Eleanor Roosevelt began doing for him what he was unable to do himself. She visited state prisons, mental hospitals and hospitals for crippled children. She learned to judge what was bad and what was good in what she saw. If, for example, beds were stacked in closets it probably meant that conditions were overcrowded and that they were being set up in the corridors at night. Printed menus sounded fine but she learned to look in the pots on the stove to see if the food cooking was the same as that listed on the menus. Reactions of the patients toward staff members who were showing her around often revealed more than routine questions. It seemed that she was continually taking trips, but it was nothing compared with what was in store for her after her husband was elected President in 1932.

The great depression was at its height when Franklin D. Roosevelt took office in March, 1933. There were many people out of work and living conditions were particularly bad. Knowing from past experience what a good reporter his wife was, the President relied on her more and more to keep him informed as to the welfare of the people. She became deeply concerned with the plight of young people and worked with Harry Hopkins and Aubrey Williams in establishing the National Youth Administration. The N.Y.A., as it became known, helped provide part-time work for students so that they could continue their education. It also provided work training in all sorts of fields for those who were no longer in school.

When war came she visited many service camps both at home and abroad. She began the practice of taking down names and addresses of boys she talked with and then getting in touch with their parents when she came home. She went to England, the Pacific and the Caribbean. She visited mental hospitals where there were boys whose war experiences had been more than they could endure. She visited hospitals where there were those who were badly wounded. And she learned that no matter how she felt it was friendliness, not sympathy, that these men wanted. She traveled so extensively that it is no wonder that when a code name was needed for her she was identified as "Rover."

In April, 1945, just three months after taking the oath of office for the fourth time, President Roosevelt died suddenly while spending some time at Warm Springs, Georgia.

Eleanor Roosevelt's service to her country did not end with her husband's death. Shortly after President Truman's inauguration the new President asked her to serve at the United Nations, and thus began a whole new life for her.

The trip to England aboard the *Queen Elizabeth* to the United Nations meeting was not just a pleasant ocean voyage for Mrs. Roosevelt. A large amount of her time had to be spent in reading innumerable documents that kept appearing in her stateroom—all pertaining to our government's policy concerning the United Nations.

She soon found out that Committee 3 was the one concerned with humanitarian, educational and cultural matters. It proved to be a most important group and its final report at the London meeting stirred up a great deal of controversy because it dealt with the problem of displaced war refugees from German-conquered countries who had been taken to Germany and were living in temporary camps. The committee also had to decide what was to be done with the Jewish people who had survived the German concentration camps.

The position of Russia and the countries who sided with her was that the refugees should be compelled to go back to their native countries whether they wanted to or not. If they didn't want to go they were to be treated as traitors. The position of the United States was that the displaced persons should be guaranteed the right to choose where they wanted to live. In the debate which took place before all the delegates, Mrs. Roosevelt was chosen to defend the position of the United States. When the votes were counted the decision was made as she had argued. The refugees were given the right to choose whether they would return to their former countries or not.

Years later, in 1954, Mrs. Roosevelt received the first Fridjof Nansen medal, named for the great Norwegian explorer who had worked for war refugees following World War I. It was awarded to Mrs. Roosevelt for the outstanding work she had done on Committee 3 and for the personal interest she took in the problems of refugees from that time on.

After she returned from London and the organizational meeting of the U.N. she thought her work was finished. But this was far from true. In 1946, a Committee was created by the Economic and Social Council of the United Nations to make recommendations for the Commission on Human Rights. The members of the commission were chosen as individuals rather than official representatives of their governments. Mrs. Roosevelt was asked to serve and willingly accepted. At about the same time, President Truman again asked her to serve as a United States delegate to the General Assembly of the United Nations. Her nomination was confirmed by the Senate and she served in that capacity until 1953, as long as President Truman remained in office.

Serving on the commission which wrote the Declaration of Human Rights was a task that Mrs. Roosevelt considered most important. She was appointed chairman of the commission and the writing of the Declaration took two years.

In 1948, when the General Assembly of the United Nations met in Paris, the Declaration of Human Rights was presented. It was finally accepted on December 10 after a great deal of debate.

Although Mrs. Roosevelt continued to be a member of the commission, she resigned from the chairmanship in 1951. The following year, after the election of President Eisenhower, all the delegates to the United Nations resigned so that the new President could make appointments as he wished; but Mrs. Roosevelt was so interested in the work of the United Nations that she offered her services to the American Association for the United Nations. The purpose of this organization is to keep the people of the United States informed about the aims and work of the United Nations. In connection with her work Mrs. Roosevelt travels extensively, explaining what the United Nations stands for and its efforts to preserve peace throughout the world.

In September, 1961, Mrs. Roosevelt was asked to serve as a special adviser to the United States delegation to the United Nations. At a time when every day brought a fresh crisis, the wisdom, experience, understanding and compassion of Eleanor Roosevelt could well be used.

Because of her journeys abroad, Eleanor Roosevelt's name is almost as well known in foreign countries as it is at home. And because of her great tact and graciousness when visiting other countries she is a welcome guest wherever she goes.

She feels that it is necessary to know what the individuals of other countries believe and that it is not necessary to make their ideas over to conform with ours. All of us must recognize that we are striving toward the same goals, and that we suffer from the same things—

ignorance and poverty. Just as mutual respect is needed as a basis for personal friendships, it is needed as a basis for friendship between countries.

Mrs. Roosevelt believes, too, that one should have the courage to stand up for his convictions even if it means the loss of prestige or popularity. The choice is not always easy but she thinks it is the duty of those who oppose prejudice to speak out against it.

Because of her courage and her belief that all knowledge should be used for the good of all human beings, Eleanor Roosevelt has indeed earned the title of the "World's First Lady."

Marian Anderson: ambassador of good will

"He's got you and me, brother, in His hands,
He's got you and me, sister, in His hands,
He's got everybody here in His hands,
He's got the whole world in His hands."

When Marian Anderson, the great Negro contralto, sings this spiritual, which she says is very precious to her, she gives it such deep meaning that audiences all over the world are moved whether or not they understand the words. For the appeal of music is not limited to one race, nor to the country where it had its origin. It is universal and belongs to everyone.

In 1957, the State Department, through the International Exchange Program of the American National Theatre and Academy, asked Marian Anderson to make a good-will trip to the Far East. She went not only as a singer but as an honored ambassador of America, and everywhere she went she received the highest honors. The King of Thailand, who had never been known to do such a thing before, arose from his throne and came down to meet her when she was brought into his presence. She was invited to speak before the Gandhi Memorial in Old Delhi, India, an honor never before extended to a foreigner. Everywhere she went crowds came to hear her sing and were held enthralled by her magnificent voice. She was interviewed many times and answered countless questions about conditions in the United States. Always her answers were wise and understanding.

Marian Anderson, born in 1908, was the oldest of the three daughters of John and Annie Anderson. At the time of her birth her parents were living in a rented room on Philadelphia's south side. When she was about two years old the little family moved to her grandmother's. But with the coming of little sister Alyce, still larger quarters were needed and a house was rented on Colorado Street. It was here that Ethel, the youngest child, was later born and here that Marian spent her childhood.

Mr. Anderson worked hard to provide for his family, and although there were not any luxuries, it was a happy life for all of them. Mrs. Anderson, a former schoolteacher from Virginia, believed that her place was in her home caring for her children, and as long as her husband lived, that was what she did.

The Andersons were regular church attenders and Mr. Anderson participated actively in anything he was called upon to do for his church. When Alyce and Ethel were very young, Mrs. Anderson had to stay home with them, but Marian proudly accompanied her father to church every Sunday. The congregation of Union Baptist Church can boast that it was in their church that the voice of Marian Anderson was first discovered.

Marian was only six years old when she was enrolled in the junior choir. The music director took a great deal of interest in the little girl and soon found that she was apt in learning alto parts. She sang a duet with another girl for their Sunday School and the next Sunday the director had them repeat it at the main service. This was Marian's first public appearance.

When Marian was about eight, her father bought her a secondhand piano and what joy it was to her! She also had her heart set on a violin that she had seen in a pawn shop window. It cost all of $3.98 and it took a long time for Marian to earn that much money.

She scrubbed porch steps for the neighbors and ran their errands and one proud day she took her hard-earned money and bought the violin. Unfortunately, the violin was not very good and even with the loving care it received it didn't last long.

Marian's fame as a child singer began to spread and soon other churches were asking her to sing for them at fund-raising meetings. Mr. Anderson was not very happy about this because he didn't, as he said, want his little girl "sung to death."

When Marian was ten years old tragedy came into her life. Her father was injured in an accident and died as a result. Her mother, forced to go to work, had no other alternative than to move her family back to Grandmother's. Grandmother was kind but it was her house and she was boss. She thought, as did others in the family, that Marian should stop school and go to work as soon as she was old enough. But Marian's mother was firm in her refusal to allow her to do so. She insisted that Marian was going to finish high school at least.

By the time Marian was thirteen she was singing in the adult choir of the church. She was not just singing alto parts, either. If a soprano or tenor substitute was needed she was asked to fill in. And by singing an octave higher than the music was written she could even take the baritone and bass parts. Marian didn't mind what part she was asked to do just as long as it was singing. She loved every minute of it and audiences never made her self-conscious.

One time the choir was asked to perform at a New York City church and Roland Hayes, the great Negro tenor, heard her. He was so impressed that he went to Philadelphia to try to persuade Marian's family to give her singing lessons. Grandmother said no, there was no need, and this time Grandmother won out.

But Marian went on singing, sometimes getting paid for it, and finally she decided to charge $5.00 for her services. Although Roland Hayes couldn't make Grandmother see the need of lessons, he didn't lose interest in Marian. Through him and other friends she began to get singing engagements in places outside of Philadelphia. It wasn't easy for her. Her mother still insisted that she keep on with her school work. That meant whenever she went someplace to sing she had to study twice as hard when she came back, to catch up. But all the hard work was worth while, for her growing reputation brought her to the attention of another Negro singer whose voice had been trained. Her name was Mary Saunders Patterson and she offered to help Marian free of charge. She was Marian's first teacher.

While Marian was still in high school she was taken to see Giuseppi Boghetti, a famous vocal teacher. He offered to take her as one of his students but she could not afford the lessons. It was then that Marian learned what loyal friends she had. When the people at her church learned how badly she wanted the lessons they arranged a benefit concert and presented her with the six hundred dollars that they raised. If the congregation of the Union Baptist Church can boast that Marian Anderson once sang in their choir, just so Marian can remember with gratitude that it was through them that she started her great career.

Giuseppi Boghetti was her teacher for many years. During the time she studied with him she gave many concerts but one seemed to her such a disaster that she almost gave up her plans to be a singer.

Mr. Boghetti had persuaded her to let him arrange a concert in Town Hall in New York City, but to her great disappointment the audience was small and the critics were harsh. Marian felt deflated when it was over and was so discouraged that she hardly had the courage to pick up the pieces and begin again. One of her weaknesses that the concert revealed was her lack of knowledge of foreign languages. She realized that if ever she was to have a musical career she must fully understand the language she was singing.

But if Marian was discouraged, Mr. Boghetti was not. Once again he worked to build up Marian's confidence in herself. The Lewisohn Stadium Association in New York held a competition and he persuaded Marian to enter. Out of about three hundred contestants, Marian won, which meant that she would not only receive a prize but be soloist with the New York Philharmonic Orchestra at an open air Lewisohn Stadium concert. This time the critics were more kind and praised her voice and her singing ability. Besides restoring her confidence in herself, the experience helped her in a material way: now she could command a larger fee when she was on a concert tour. And a professional management bureau asked to be her manager.

Although more and more concert offers were coming in, Marian was not satisfied. She had felt for some time that she would like to study in Europe, and now she proceeded to carry through her plans. Her first trip was to London. She stayed almost a year and then came home to earn more money so she could go back.

Her second trip was to Germany. Living with a German family

and studying at the same time, she grew more proficient in the language she felt was necessary for her to know in order to interpret the German songs she enjoyed singing.

From Germany she went to Norway to give some concerts. She was received very well there but she felt her audiences were curious as well as musically minded. They were not accustomed to Negroes and were interested in seeing and knowing one firsthand.

Tours in Sweden and Finland followed, and in Finland two important things happened. Marian acquired a Finnish accompanist, Kosti Vehanen, who was to stay with her for many years, and Finland's great composer, Jean Sibelius, received her in his home, where she sang for him. He was so impressed with her singing that he later dedicated one of his compositions, "Solitude," to her.

After another concert tour in the United States she returned to Europe for two more years of triumph, singing in London, Paris, Brussels, Geneva, Vienna, Salzberg and other cities. At a concert in Paris, Sol Hurok, considered one of the finest managers in the United States, heard her sing and offered her a contract. Her American reputation was now ensured.

Marian's first concert in New York after her European trip was to be in Town Hall where she had failed before. It looked as though Fate was still not on her side, for on the home-bound ship she fell and broke her ankle. It seemed that the concert might have to be cancelled, but Marian assured her manager that she could go through with it. With sheer grit she managed to appear on the stage, her foot in a cast and concealed by her long gown. Not until the concert was half over did the enthusiastic audience realize what had happened to her. This time the critics were extremely complimentary, and Mr. Hurok immediately arranged for a Carnegie Hall concert, the goal of every American artist.

In 1936, Miss Anderson was invited to sing in Russia. She had been warned not to include any religious songs in her concerts but she disregarded that warning and sang "Ave Maria" and the Negro spirituals for which she was so famous. Her audiences cheered her and demanded encore after encore.

After she came back to the United States, Mr. Hurok attempted to secure a concert for her in Constitution Hall in Washington. But he was unable to arrange one because the building, owned by the

Daughters of the American Revolution, had never been open to members of Miss Anderson's race. When this situation became known, a great furore arose. Secretary of the Interior Harold Ickes arranged for Marian to give a concert on Easter Sunday on the steps of the Lincoln Memorial. Thousands of people attended that open-air concert and those who heard it would never forget it. Many high government officials attended, not only to hear Marian sing but also to pay tribute to her as a person.

Unhappy as the incident was, it had a happy ending. The policy for the use of Constitution Hall was changed. Later, Marian Anderson was invited to give a concert there and she accepted. Since that time other Negro artists have also appeared there.

When Marian was in high school she had met Orpheus H. Fisher, who later became an architect. Over the years they continued seeing each other whenever she was in the United States, but they were not married until 1943. Their home is a remodeled farmhouse in rural Connecticut, where, when she is not on tour, Marian can garden and cook to her heart's content.

There was to be another "first" for Marian Anderson. One night in September, 1954, she and her husband were invited to a party at Sol Hurok's, where she met Rudolf Bing, general manager of the Metropolitan Opera Company. He invited Miss Anderson to sing at the Metropolitan in the role of Ulrica, the old sorceress, in Verdi's *The Masked Ball*. On January 7, 1955, Marian became the first Negro to sing as a regular member of the Metropolitan Opera Company.

In 1958, President Dwight D. Eisenhower appointed Miss Anderson an alternate delegate to the United Nations. She served there during the years 1958 and 1959. Her work was mostly with Committee 3, which deals with social, humanitarian and cultural problems.

As a member of a minority race in the United States, Marian Anderson well understands what such problems involve. But she is not a fighter. She believes that what is needed is understanding between the races. She feels that everyone should be judged as a person, and when discrimination against her has been evident she has not shown bitterness. She feels that hate restricts and destroys a person and keeps him from growing, and she has the utmost faith in the ability of her fellow Americans to solve their racial differences in a peaceful manner.

Someone once asked Marian Anderson what her greatest moment was. There were many times she might have remembered: the Washington concert at the Lincoln Memorial; the concert at Salzberg when Toscanini, the great conductor, told her she had a voice heard only once in a century; the evening she was the invited guest of President and Mrs. Franklin D. Roosevelt at the White House to meet the King and Queen of England; her Far-East journey for the State Department; her appointment to the United Nations by President Dwight D. Eisenhower; being given the Spingarn medal in 1942 by the National Association for the Advancement of Colored People, for having done most to better relations between the races; her awards by the governments of Sweden and Finland; the honorary degrees bestowed on her by Howard University, Temple University, Smith College, Carlisle College, Moravian College and Dickinson College; being given the Bok award which is presented to a Philadelphian who has done some service that brings credit to the city; the night of her debut as a singer with the Metropolitan Opera. She might have given any of these as her greatest moment. But she didn't. Her greatest moment, said Marian Anderson, was when she told her mother she needn't work any more. For, to her mother, whom she has always revered, Marian Anderson gives the credit for the spiritual and religious guidance which has given balance to her life.

Marian Anderson, modest, talented and understanding, has well served her country and her race, at home and abroad, as an "Ambassador of Good Will."

Mahatma Gandhi: champion of the oppressed

A slight young Hindu lawyer sat in the first-class compartment of a train out of Durban, South Africa. He was on his way to Pretoria to argue the case of a client, and spread out on his knees were papers he was reviewing on the case. He was wearing a neat western-style suit and had removed his turban because of the heat in the train. He looked the typical British traveler with nothing to mark him as different— except the color of his skin! The train stopped at a station, the door to the compartment suddenly opened, and a traveler with white skin stared at him for a moment, slammed the door and left. In a very short time the door was reopened and the man again stood there, this time accompanied by a railroad officer.

"You will have to go back to the third-class carriage," he was told.

The Hindu responded by showing the officer his first-class ticket.

"It makes no difference. You cannot ride first class. I advise you to go at once unless you want to be forced off the train."

The young lawyer became indignant. "I was sold a first-class ticket at Durban to ride this train. I will ride first class or not at all, in which case you will have to use force to put me off."

The officer glared at the dark-skinned man for only a moment. Then suddenly, with no further word, he picked up the Hindu's bags and threw them on the platform, seized the Hindu and thrust him off the train. The train pulled out and was gone. The little man looked dejectedly at his luggage, then went into the cold unheated station to ponder what had happened.

The Hindu who was stranded was Mohandas Gandhi. He had been educated in England and admitted to the bar to practice law and, after several years' experience in his native India, had accepted a position in Durban, South Africa. Since his arrival in Africa he had noticed with what contempt the Indians were treated by the white man. And now this episode of being thrown off a train when he had a perfectly good ticket was an insult not only to his race but to himself as an individual. Inside the station he sat for hours trying to make up his mind what to do. Should he continue to fight for his rights and go on to Pretoria to complete his work? Or should he throw all his plans to the wind and return to India? He decided to stay. Gandhi didn't realize it then, but the decision he made that day in the railway station was to affect hundreds of millions of people. His fight for the rights of the Indian population in South Africa was to continue for twenty years, after which the stage would change to his native India, for the struggle of his own people. Gandhi was to become famous as the savior of India, champion of equality and peace. Strangely enough, the kind of fight he would make would become synonomous with the word peace, not only in India but the rest of the world. He was to become the instigator of the largest force for peaceful, nonviolent rebellion the world had ever known. Although he had adopted western dress as a student, he would soon become known as the little brown man in the simple, white cotton garments of ancient Hindu custom. He would forever be associated with the *charka,* or spinning wheel, a symbol of rebellion against imported British cloth. His simple diet of fruits, nuts and goat's milk and his fasts and periodic silences would become a part of the man who punished himself for the shortcomings of others. Most important, the creed of universal love he preached and practiced would lead his country to freedom and cut the shackles of the caste system that had prevailed in India for thousands of years. This was the man who became Mahatma, the Great-Souled One, to many millions of people.

Mohandas Gandhi was born in 1869 into a family of middle caste, the youngest of five children. In accordance with the ancient Hindu religion practiced strictly by his family, Mohandas was betrothed soon after birth and was married when he was thirteen years old. (He and his wife Kasturbai lived together sixty-two years until her death in prison at his side.) As a boy Mohandas had the greatest respect for his father and tried always to please him. One night after the boy had been conscience-stricken by some sin he had committed, he wrote out a confession of guilt and gave it to his father. As the father read it the tears fell from his eyes. Gandhi later wrote of this incident, "Those pearl drops of love cleansed my heart and washed my sin away." He was also deeply impressed by his devout mother, who often accompanied her prayers with fasting.

When he was nineteen he went to England for three years of study. After being admitted to the bar he eventually accepted a position in South Africa obtained for him by his brother.

As a barrister, Gandhi found it difficult to overcome his shyness, which often made him tongue-tied when he spoke in public. When at last he learned to speak eloquently, he still retained a simplicity and directness of speech that touched the hearts of his listeners as no flowery phrases could have done.

When he went to Africa he expected to stay a year, but something happened that convinced him he should remain to carry on his fight for the Indians there. As he was about to leave to go back to

India, he was handed a newspaper telling about a bill that was about to pass through the legislature which would make it impossible for Indians in the Natal to be elected to the Assembly. He stayed to fight the bill until it was overruled by English law.

He began to publish a periodical called *Indian Opinion*. In it, he voiced his views frankly and urged the Indian population to stand up for their rights to self-respect. Through his newspaper, many persons became aware of the outspoken Hindu who was becoming a leader among his people. Gandhi had arrived in South Africa in 1892. During the twenty years that he stayed there he established his first non-violence method of resistance. It was called *"satyagraha."*

The word *satyagraha* was derived from the Indian words *saty*—truth, and *agraha*—force. In 1906, Gandhi led a crusade against discriminative legislation that oppressed the Indian population. His two thousand followers in the crusade practiced passive resistance by refusing to comply with the unfair laws. The *satyagrahis* were trained at the *ashram,* a sort of plantation, outside of Johannesburg which had been given to them by one of Gandhi's followers. Gandhi had named the place Tolstoy Farm because of his great admiration for Count Tolstoy, the Russian writer and champion of the peasants. The *ashram* was a self-sustaining farm where Gandhi's disciples lived in the utmost simplicity, raising their own food, grinding their own flour, weaving their cloth and making their shoes. They practiced strict frugality in their diets, for all who were assembled there were fully aware that eventually they would be imprisoned for their resistance to the British law. And they were, time and time again.

After seven years of patient but persistent resistance during which Gandhi and his *satyagrahis* were arrested many times, the Indian Relief Bill was passed in July, 1914, giving the Indians much that they had fought for. It reversed the law that Indian marriages were illegal; it brought to an end the importation of indentured Indian labor, and eliminated the poll tax on Indian laborers; and it provided that Indians born in South Africa might enter the Cape Colony.

When the Relief Bill was passed, Gandhi knew that his work in Africa was finished. He returned home to India.

Gandhi had always hoped that India would become an independent nation. Even as a young man, he had been conscious of the fact that his native country, though it was inhabited by more than three hundred million Indians, was after all under the domination of the British with an army to enforce their rule. Gandhi believed that the same nonviolent resistance as that used in South Africa, if employed by Indians in their own country could—if it were strong enough—secure freedom for India. And so Gandhi's "nonviolent non-cooperation" policy was begun. Under his leadership, British goods were boycotted; Indians deserted the British army; children left British schools; Indians turned in all medals and honors they had received from the British. Spinning wheels suddenly became symbols of Gandhi's aim at self-reliance because they demonstrated the people's determination to weave their own cloth instead of importing it from Britain.

The movement swept over India like an epidemic. India for the Indians! The people hung on every word that was uttered by the Mahatma, the Great-Souled One. But the huge majority were ignorant and uneducated in political understanding. They loved their leader, but many of them could not grasp the meaning of the message he taught: "My noncooperation has its roots not in hatred but in love." And because some of them didn't understand, they performed acts of violence in which British were killed, with the result that thirty thousand Indians were put into prison. Gandhi was bowed with grief at the violence—so far from what he had intended. He felt responsible for the hatred his people had shown toward their enemies. He realized that the movement had grown too fast and he called off the noncooperation plan. He wanted the Indian people to understand why the resistance must take the form of nonviolence—that the love of God could be realized "only by wishing harm to no one, not even the British." While the Mahatma prayed and fasted as he struggled with his problem, the authorities came to arrest him. In court he said that he'd had to take the choice of either giving in to a system which was unfair to his people, or taking the risk that they might go beyond his orders of nonviolence. He had risked the latter, and he was sorry. He said that he knew the court's only recourse was to punish him. The judge, with some reluctance, sentenced him to six years' imprisonment. Two years later, in 1924, he was released by a British labor government.

During all his life, Gandhi fought another evil which, to almost anyone else living in his part of the world, would have seemed a hopeless battle. This was the very strong and very ancient caste system. Gandhi, in his infinite wisdom and high hope for the equality of men, hated caste. He knew that it had existed for several thousand years, that it had been brought to India by conquering tribes of Aryans, that it was an integral part of the Hindu religion, and that it was recognized by the British authorities. But Gandhi believed that the caste system was against God's will and that India must give it up!

The caste system is so complex that it would be almost impossible for the average Westerner to understand it. Indians were born into a caste to which they would belong until the day they died. There were four castes and these were divided into several thousand subcastes. It was against the Hindu religion to marry outside one's caste, and most desirable to marry within the subcaste. When a son was born the parents tried to arrange for a suitable marriage for him within the subcaste. The top caste was composed of Brahmans, those eligible to be educated as priests or teachers. Below, scaled downward, were the soldiers, the craftsmen, the merchants and farmers and—last—the common laborers in field and factory. But those for whom Gandhi was most concerned were the out-castes, the poor souls who were born without any caste at all. These were known as the "untouchables" but Gandhi called them the Children of God. Nowhere in the world were human beings treated with such contempt as these pitiful creatures who had no rights, no possessions and no decent way of livelihood. They were allowed to live only on the fringes of a town or village, and never permitted to mingle with the townspeople. Their role in life was to do the most menial labor, such as removing dead bodies of men and animals, clearing up refuse and human wastes, and cleaning the streets. It was demanded that they live a life apart. They could not touch anything a caste Hindu touched. So fierce were the laws protecting the caste Hindus from the untouchables that in some provinces a warning sound was given to tell them to clear the road because a caste Hindu was approaching. If an untouchable by some chance touched a caste Hindu or even if only his shadow fell upon the other, then the caste Hindu must purge himself by a carefully prescribed ritual of cleansing. All this was a part of the ancient Hindu religion which included a belief in reincarnation. It was believed that the untouchables were paying for sins committed in some previous incarnation.

The untouchables were the piteous objects of Gandhi's fight against oppression. He showed his scorn of the system by mingling with them, employing them to work in his home and even to prepare his food. He went further when he adopted an untouchable as his own daughter and brought other homeless orphan Children of God into his home to live.

Even his own devout followers found it hard at first to accept the out-castes as equals. But when Gandhi set an example by doing such chores as cleaning the lavatories of the *ashram,* a task done heretofore only by untouchables, they followed his lead. When all performed the same kind of duties, caste was eliminated in the *ashram.* When the thousands of high-caste Indians who visited Gandhi through the years saw the untouchables treated as equals, much of the curse of the out-castes was lost. The people revered their leader so greatly that eventually the laws against the untouchables were repealed.

"All my life," Gandhi wrote some years later, "I have stood for the minorities and those in need." His championing of the untouchables had been the means of overcoming an ancient and leprous custom that had been the great sore spot of India.

Another of Gandhi's problems was to try to break down the thick wall that existed between Hindus and Moslems. The two religious factions were almost constantly struggling against each other, causing riots and bloodshed. Gandhi had always preached religious tolerance. In the *ashram,* Hindus and Moslems lived side by side, working and studying together. When fighting occurred in India between the people of the two religions, Gandhi took their sins upon himself. At one time after fighting had become serious, he decided to punish himself for their follies. He entered upon a twenty-one day period of fasting and prayer, and kept his vow not to touch food. As he grew weaker, his friends argued with him to take a sip of milk. He answered them by writing on paper (in order to keep his vow of silence also), "Where is your faith in God? You have forgotten the power of prayer." The people of India watched and prayed with him and became frightened when the Mahatma grew frailer and weaker. When he was near the point of death they could stand it no longer. They couldn't let him die. So they made peace and promised him tolerance for each other's religion. Although this episode would not forever settle all differences between them, the Hindus and Moslems learned one thing from it: that their great leader was ready at any moment to lay down his life for their good.

Gandhi always hoped to unite the Moslems and Hindus and was very unhappy when it was decided to partition India into two separate states. But the new provisional government was formed in September, 1946. Then great violence broke out in Calcutta and five thousand people were killed. He started for Calcutta, crossing India in a slow-moving train with thousands lining the way to cheer him on. Just before he arrived, terrible riots there took a toll of ten thousand dead.

Arriving in Calcutta, the Mahatma started his last march, walking through the villages in his white cotton garments, often barefoot, staying in each village for a few days to talk to the people and try to quiet their fears. He reminded them of the brotherhood of men, and urged forgiveness in their hearts for those who were their enemies. Before his pilgrimage was over, conditions were greatly improved and the turmoil had quieted down.

On March 22, 1947, Lord Mountbatten, Britain's last viceroy to India, arrived in Delhi and asked Gandhi and Jinnah (the leader of the Moslems) to meet with him at the palace. Independence had come and affairs must be settled and the terms fixed for partition. But peace had not yet come among the people. Fighting was still going on. On January 13th, Gandhi, in protest against the riots, entered on his last fast. "How long will I fast?" he said. "Until peace comes and the people of all religions in India mix like brothers."

At the end of five days, the frail tiny man was so weak that the people in the streets prayed openly for his life. But on that day a pledge of peace was made between the Hindu and Moslem leaders.

Twelve days later when Gandhi, now very frail and old, was brought to the garden where he had been holding a prayer meeting each evening, he was shot and killed by a fanatic who opposed conciliation.

The Great-Souled One was gone, but what would live on was the spirit of the little brown man who conquered not by the sword but by love.

Alfred Nobel and the Nobel Peace Prize

Alfred Nobel was born in Stockholm, Sweden, in 1833. When he was nine years old his family moved to St. Petersburg, now Leningrad, Russia. His childhood was tormented by ill health, and after the move to Russia his only schooling as a child was the instruction he received at home from his mother; but he became an avid reader of all kinds of books and even learned several languages. He had always been interested in the history of European countries, and when he was nineteen his father sent him on a two-year tour of Europe and the United States. He finished his education in the United States, where he studied under the famous engineer, John Ericsson, inventor of the warship *Monitor*.

Alfred's interest in engineering and chemistry were encouraged by the fact that his father was an inventor. With Alfred's older brothers, Immanuel Nobel was in the chemical manufacturing business. But the business in St. Petersburg failed and the family returned to Sweden. As a young man, Alfred did extensive research in his father's factory. In the process of manufacturing and shipping nitroglycerine, there were so many serious accidents that the Nobels were considered public enemies of mankind to have put such a potent explosive on the market. Finally, in 1867, Alfred Nobel was successful in combining nitroglycerine with another substance that made it safe for handling and shipping. He patented his invention, calling it Dynamite.

The new explosive sold rapidly in countries all over the world, and Alfred Nobel became a very wealthy man. But in spite of the fact that he had money for every luxury, he was not a happy man. He had never married and he spent much of his time alone. As he grew older he became very nervous and had increasingly poor health. He saw his invention being used for destructive purposes in times of war, when he had meant it for peacetime use. His thoughts turned more and more to an idealistic future when all of Europe might be at peace. In 1893, he wrote in a letter to a friend that he was thinking of establishing a peace prize "to the man or woman who has done the most to advance the idea of general peace."

In November, 1895, Alfred Nobel put his idea into concrete form by making his will and leaving his immense fortune to form a trust fund. The interest was to be used for prizes which would be awarded "to those persons who, during the previous year, have rendered the greatest services to mankind." He stipulated that five prizes should be awarded annually: one for outstanding work in physics, one for chemistry, one for medicine, one for literature, and the fifth "to the person who has done the most or best work for the brotherhood of nations, the abolition or reduction of standing armies, as well as the formation or popularization of peace congresses." He stipulated that the prizes should be awarded without regard to the nationality of the candidates.

Alfred Nobel died the following year, leaving a fund of nine million dollars for the Nobel Prizes. The interest would amount to about forty thousand dollars for each prize. After his death, the machinery was set in motion to form committees for awarding the prizes. The first prizes were awarded in 1901 and with few exceptions they have been awarded annually ever since. Winners of the peace prize, like those in the other categories, have been of many nationalities and from many walks of life.

In 1935, the winner was Carl von Ossietzky, a German pacifist who was a prisoner of the Nazis when the prize was awarded.

In 1960, a Zulu chief, Albert Luthuli of South Africa, won the peace prize for his work in organizing the nonviolent "sit-in" crusade to oppose segregation in South Africa. Although the government deposed him and banished him to his home district, it permitted him and his wife to go to Oslo, Norway, to accept the prize. Luthuli was the first African to receive a Nobel award.

In 1961, the peace prize was awarded posthumously for the first time, to Dag Hammarskjold, Secretary-General of the United Nations, who had lost his life while on a peace mission in the Congo.

Sometimes two persons have been awarded the prize jointly, and on several occasions organizations have won the coveted award for their outstanding work for peace.

The peace prize also has been awarded for special projects. In 1906, Theodore Roosevelt was the first American to receive it, for the part he played in negotiating peace in the Russo-Japanese War. In 1934, Arthur Henderson, a British diplomat, won the coveted award for his work as president of the World Disarmament Conference. Because he helped to organize international labor unions, Leon Jouhaux of France received it in 1951. And in 1957 it was bestowed on Lester B. Pearson, a Canadian, for his work for the United Nations in keeping peace in Egypt.

These are just a few examples of the type of activity for which the Peace Prize, founded by the Swedish idealist Alfred Nobel, has been awarded through the years.

part **VII**
LEADING TO BROTHERHOOD

LEADING TO BROTHERHOOD

*We have learned that we cannot live
alone in peace; that our well-being is dependent on the well-being of other nations far away . . . We have learned the
simple truth, as Emerson said, that "the
only way to have a friend is to be one."*
—FRANKLIN DELANO ROOSEVELT

We have dealt with some of the well-known individuals and organizations that have helped pave the road toward understanding. In this
final section, we will talk about people—some of them among the
readers of this book—whose services range through many fields:
scientists who risk their lives for human knowledge in the freezing tem-
peratures of Antarctica; artists who share their talents throughout the
world; contributors of large sums of money in gestures of good will—
even letter writers who form world friendships through faithful correspondence. Each of their efforts, large or small, gives true meaning
to the word BROTHERHOOD.

The story of the
National Conference of Christians and Jews

The Declaration of Independence states that "all men are created equal, that they are endowed by their Creator with certain unalienable rights, that among these are Life, Liberty and the pursuit of Happiness."

Unfortunately, all the citizens living under this great declaration have not believed in it. Prejudice has always existed among some people of our nation, and one form of it is prejudice against people of other faiths.

In the late nineteen-twenties a growing number of influential people wanted to start a movement that would advance the idea of brotherhood among men of different faiths. Their interest in such a movement was the beginning of the National Conference of Christians and Jews. Although the organization began with neither a director nor a definite program and was nurtured at a time when religious bigotry was apparent in many phases of American life, still its founders had great faith in it. In 1928 the organization came into being under the leadership of Charles Evans Hughes, Secretary of State; Newton D. Baker, former Secretary of War; and S. Parkes Cadman, famous clergyman and lecturer. They secured Dr. Everett R. Clinchy, a young Presbyterian minister, to direct their program. Dr. Clinchy was a firm believer in a brotherhood that included a tolerance for all religious faiths, and a democracy where all men are brothers regardless of their religious differences.

Money is needed to develop any new movement, and this one was backed financially by Roger Williams Straus. Mr. Straus had learned religious tolerance early from his father, the famous Jewish-American statesman, Oscar S. Straus. The senior Straus had written a book in 1894 entitled *Roger Williams, the Pioneer of Religious Liberty*. Roger Straus was ready to give full support to this new National Conference to educate people in tolerance. He served, with John Herring, as first associate chairman.

The Conference grew slowly at first, but its charter members of Protestants, Catholics and Jews, joining together for the first time, were determined to see it succeed. First of all they sought to protect the rights of each other, and, setting the goal high, were determined to "make nothing less than world brotherhood a reality." According to their bylaws, they seek to "promote justice, amity, understanding and cooperation among Protestants, Catholics and Jews in the United States and to analyze, moderate and finally eliminate inter-group prejudices which disfigure and distort religious, business, social and political relations."

The first seminar of the new association took place at Columbia University in January, 1929 with talks by Columbia President Nicholas Murray Butler; Father J. Elliot Ross, Catholic student adviser at Columbia University; and Rabbi Isaac Landman, editor of *The American Hebrew*. In the panel discussion that followed, Rabbi Landman made a significant remark that expressed what was to become a basic aim of the organization. Each man who rose to his feet had declared his firm convictions in his own particular form of religion. "Therefore," said Rabbi Landman, *"the problem is to agree to disagree agreeably."*

In October, 1933, a seven-weeks tour to sell brotherhood was undertaken by Dr. Clinchy, Father Ross and Rabbi Morris S. Lazaron of Baltimore. Together they traveled nine thousand miles, visiting thirty-eight cities in twenty-one states. Called the "Tolerance Trio," they appeared on platforms together, discussing their religions and then their everyday problems in common, as Americans in particular and human beings in general.

When the plans for this tour had been made known, protests from all sides came to the three participants to discourage their enterprise. But the trio remained firm in their intent and the tour was a great success. Their very first stop, in Baltimore, ended up with the formation of a Baltimore branch of NCCJ, and in Dallas, Texas, a South-western division was started. From coast to coast the three were welcomed by interested and enthusiastic audiences.

BROTHERHOOD WEEK

Many people worked hard to contribute to the spread of the ideals of brotherhood to which the National Conference of Christians and Jews was dedicated. One idea for furthering the cause and helping it to become known throughout America came from Father Hugh L. McMenamin, a priest of Denver, Colorado. At a two-day seminar in 1931, he made the suggestion for a National Goodwill Week to be held annually. Finally, in 1934, the NCCJ announced that a national "Brotherhood Day" would be observed on the last Sunday in April. The purposes in observing a special day were made clear when the NCCJ stated, "The day is not to deal with doctrinal differences. It will not promote worship. It will not suggest a weakening of anyone's religious convictions. It will deal with our relationships as citizens. The plans will suggest that the energies of Americans should be turned away from prejudice and toward joint constructive efforts . . . Brotherhood Day will make use of educational approaches to the problems of human relationships."

The idea was met not only with approval but with promises of co-operation from people of all faiths from every section of the country. President Franklin Delano Roosevelt endorsed Brotherhood Day and invited all the American people, regardless of race or religion, to take part in its observance.

The slogan chosen for the first Brotherhood Day was, "Make America Safe for Differences." In spite of the limited amount of publicity that had preceded the day, it was observed by civic meetings in more than three hundred communities at which Protestants, Catholics and Jews took part, and was celebrated widely by schools and churches.

The idea caught on. By the following year it was observed in about one thousand communities and was featured by such organizations as the YMCA, the Boy Scouts, B'nai B'rith and the Service Bureau for Education in Human Relations. Schools and colleges put on brotherhood programs in which Protestant, Catholic and Jewish students took part. Each year, the day was observed by more and more communities with so many cooperating programs that, five years after it was inaugurated, Brotherhood Day became Brotherhood Week. It was decided that it should always be celebrated in the week that included Washington's birthday.

When Harold E. Stassen became General Chairman of Brotherhood Week in 1946, he foresaw that the action of and promotion for the Conference could no longer be confined just to one week. Thereafter, promoting the movement toward brotherhood was a year-round program for NCCJ.

The 1946 Brotherhood Week has been called the "largest mass education program ever undertaken by any civic group." Some of the activities for promoting it that year were coast-to-coast radio programs, an extensive advertising campaign put on by the Advertising Council, a movie entitled *The American Creed,* put on by the Motion Picture Division for American Brotherhood, countless newspaper and magazine articles and stories, and many hundreds of church, school and college programs that were produced in communities across the nation.

And so each succeeding year saw the education of the public in the interest of brotherhood expanding, until there was scarcely an organization in America that was not aware of it or cooperating with it. As one writer expressed it, "America is better today and stronger because of Brotherhood Week." When the NCCJ had started, there was a great deal of criticism of it from those who said it wouldn't work. For a time, in its early days, it had had to close up its office for lack of funds; but by the very nature of its virtues, the idea had to succeed. The small staff grew larger as the movement progressed, and the offices required more and more space. In 1955 the headquarters in New York moved into its own building, the Building for Brotherhood, a gift of the Ford Motors Fund and the three Ford brothers.

There has been a tremendous growth of community action in cooperation since the organization was first established. When the Tolerance Trio set out in 1933 to talk of brotherhood to United States citizens, they were faced with opposition and suspicion. In later years the situation became very different. Far from having to "sell" brotherhood, the NCCJ has a year-round task to fill the requests that come in constantly for program helps and materials, from civic clubs, YMCA's and YWCA's, Boy Scouts and Girl Scouts, churches and synogogues, schools and colleges in all the fifty states. The dream of the founders, to make every American conscious of brotherhood, is becoming a reality.

WORLD BROTHERHOOD

Even before World War II was over, leaders at NCCJ in the United States were thinking of European organizations for brotherhood. Fresh in the minds of the world were the Anti-Semitic crimes of Adolf Hitler in which six million Jews were exterminated. At no time in history had there been such a campaign of hate and intolerance. In the National Conference of Christians and Jews, men knew that the time was ripe, the need was now, and the job tremendous. But, as Mr. Arthur H. Compton told his colleagues at a meeting of NCCJ, "In the postwar world, our contacts must be world contacts. The principles of the National Conference must be projected on a world scale."

When the war was over and the United States sent aid to the war-torn countries of Europe, the NCCJ representatives went with them. Though they had no definite plans at the time, they knew that morale in these suffering nations was low and encouragement was needed. There must be a way for people to regain faith in each other and in the future. Although the NCCJ had had eighteen years of experience in bridging great gaps between groups of different cultures and faiths, they were well aware that the problems in Europe would be far greater than any they had faced before. Here there were differences of language, politics, cultures and traditions.

But a beginning was made. In 1946, one hundred and fifty people met at a seven-day conference in Oxford, England. They were representatives of fifteen countries from Protestant, Roman and Orthodox Catholic, and Jewish communities. The theme was "Freedom, Justice and Responsibility." The members resolved to protest attacks on any one group by any other group. At the close of the conference, a petition was drawn up and presented to the Paris Peace Conference which was then in session. The petition sought the Peace Conference's strong support of the principles contained in the United Nations Charter, which called for "fundamental freedom for all, without distinction of race, sex, language or religion."

The following year a second conference was held in Switzerland.

While the immediate problem was the care and rehabilitation of displaced Jews, there were also long-range plans made for full cooperation with the United Nations.

The National Conference was able to accomplish a great deal in Germany through educational techniques. Thirty thousand books were collected and sent to Germany to replace those burned by the Nazis. For several years the Conference sponsored the visits of several hundred German religious leaders to the United States to study American life in action. Another milestone was reached when NCCJ representatives held conferences with the Pope and other Catholic leaders, with leaders of the Jewish religion and with members of the World Council of Churches. All of this was groundwork for establishing a World Brotherhood Council and in 1950 two hundred and fifty people met in Paris to do just that. Representatives from fifteen nations began work on the charter and on the program that would be needed. The world organization had made a start.

Since that beginning, chapters of the World Brotherhood Council have been established in all countries of Western Europe and in North Africa. Like its parent organization, NCCJ in America, the vision was broad and the problems were many. Since the end of World War II, billions of dollars have been spent on material helps and redevelopment programs for our ever-changing, competitive world, but no price can be set on the ideals demonstrated by the work of the National Conference of Christians and Jews and the Council of World Brotherhood. Their goal is to help all peoples everywhere to believe in the brotherhood of man. As President Harry S. Truman once said, "The cultivation of the spirit of brotherhood is merely the fulfillment of the purpose of God that all His children should live together as one family."

The Rockefeller and Ford Foundations: brotherhood through education

Webster's Dictionary defines a foundation as "an endowed institution, corporation or charity." There are many foundations, some large, some small, which have been established in an effort to help people either individually or nationally. Some deal with work of special interest to their founders. Some are established to help worthy persons in whatever field of work they have chosen. Two of these Foundations, the Rockefeller and the Ford, because of their widespread endeavors and also because of the large sums of money they have spent, have become internationally known.

THE ROCKEFELLER FOUNDATION

The older of the two Foundations is the Rockefeller Foundation. Although John D. Rockefeller had formerly made large contributions to the promotion of welfare and science, it was in 1909 that he established a trust fund to be known as the Rockefeller Foundation. He did this by turning over to three persons, one of whom was his son, John D. Rockefeller, Jr., shares of stock in the Standard Oil Company valued at fifty million dollars. In the deed of trust he issued, he set forth as the purposes of the Foundation to acquire and impart knowledge in the prevention and relief of suffering and to promote human progress by all possible means. It is interesting to know that by 1960 the work had expanded so that the board of trustees numbered twenty-four persons and that in addition there were twenty-nine officers and directors.

When the Rockefeller Foundation was first established, Mr. Rockefeller's idea was that the money should be given to continue projects already started which would not discontinue when they no longer received funds from the Foundation. He wanted to encourage in the institutions he helped a spirit of self-reliance and independence.

One of his early interests had been medical research, and as early as 1901 the Rockefeller Institute for Medical Research had been founded. It is not surprising that this interest has continued in the work of the Rockefeller Foundation throughout the years. In 1960, out of nearly thirty-three million dollars spent by the Foundation during that year, over ten million dollars was in the fields of medical and natural sciences.

In 1909, work in public health had been relatively undeveloped. One of the first studies the Foundation interested itself in was the eradication of hookworm. This was a disease about which little was known even though it had disabling effects on its victims. Education in sanitation was necessary to bring about its control in the parts of the world where it was prevalent.

Another research activity begun in 1915 and continued for many years was the fight against yellow fever. Although much was learned about this dread disease by Dr. Walter Reed during the Spanish-American War and the building of the Panama Canal, there was still much to be done. The high point in the Foundation's research program was reached when a vaccine was developed to protect people against yellow fever as they are protected against smallpox.

A third disease studied by the Medical Institutes of the Foundation was malaria. In this world of rapid plane transportation malaria has been carried to parts of the world where it has never been prevalent before because the carrier of the disease is a certain species of mosquito. With the cooperation of the countries where this mosquito breeds, fumigating areas were established and planes leaving airports were carefully dusted with disinfectant before taking off. Breeding spots were also sprayed, which kept malaria epidemics at a minimum.

Although the Foundation was successful in controlling epidemics in these three areas, it was decided that it was unsatisfactory to attack each disease separately. Therefore the Foundation began, instead, to support medical institutions, both old and new, whose leadership was anxious to do a better job in teaching and in research, and where there was the will and the vision to carry the plans through.

Medicine, however, has not been the only concern of the Foundation. Since many diseases develop where there is an inadequate food supply, the Foundation has been interested in improving agricultural practices, especially in the underdeveloped countries.

In Africa, research is being carried on in the fields of plant breeding, animal nutrition and the control of diseases attacking the farmers' livestock. There are agricultural programs being carried on in Mexico, South America, India and other countries.

The Rockefeller Foundation realizes that the success of the new nations of the world depends not only on the help they receive from the outside but on the education of their own citizens. Making it possible for the young men and women of these countries to study abroad is not the only answer to their problems at home, even though it adds to the students' knowledge. It is important that the leaders-to-be of the new countries be trained to understand and to solve their own problems. To achieve this objective, training centers have been set up in some of the new countries and previously established universities have been granted additional sums to train students how to help their own people.

Recognizing, too, that books and materials are woefully inadequate and unavailable in many places, the Foundation has been building up the libraries. The publications given to such institutions include those on economics, government, law, politics and world geography. Along with the individual volumes the libraries receive a set of the *Encyclopedia Britannica* and an outright gift of two thousand dollars.

The Rockefeller Foundation has also made available vast sums for all phases of education and research in the United States. It seeks to aid projects that will benefit our own country and at the same time contribute knowledge to help all mankind.

THE FORD FOUNDATION

Nowadays it is common to pick up almost any well-known magazine and find articles illustrated with pictures of students or workers from other countries living in American homes and working in American industries or on American farms. It is just as common to read of American students and workers attending universities in other countries or working side-by-side with their counterparts in another land. Much of this exchange activity is made possible through the Ford Foundation.

The Ford Foundation was chartered in 1936. During its first fifteen years it carried on its operations as many other local charities did, contributing to local institutions in which members of the Ford family were interested. The disbursement of its funds was handled by a few persons. Then in 1950 the picture changed. Through bequests left by the estates of Henry and Edsel Ford, it became a national institution devoted to the welfare of mankind. Its board of trustees now numbers fifteen, with large program and administrative staffs in addition.

Its first step before deciding on its program was to make a survey of the country, consulting leaders in all fields of endeavor as to how it could benefit the most people. When it had completed this survey, the Ford Foundation outlined its objectives. Its program, however, has always remained flexible enough so it could be adapted to any urgent need that might arise.

Many of the grants the Ford Foundation makes are well known to students. Because it is important to have well-educated leaders for the future, the National Merit Scholarship was established to help talented young people secure a college education. With the growing need for superior educational methods, special grants have been made to those working for advanced degrees, to improve the quality of their teaching. Besides grants to individuals, the Ford Foundation gave colleges and universities over two hundred and sixty million dollars within ten years to help raise faculty salaries.

Outside the field of education, money has been given to institutions working on the problems of the aged and of juvenile delinquency. Aid has also been extended toward the recruitment of talented persons to serve at all levels of government. The problems of urban and regional development have not been neglected and support has been given to studies on those subjects.

Although the greater part of the Ford Foundation grants are for aid to American institutions, the Foundation recognizes that American destiny is closely bound to that of other countries.

Almost twenty per cent of its total grants are now being made in the international field. Ford Foundation training and research activity is going on in fifty-two countries of the world. Since most projects take a long time to complete, the grants are made on a long-term basis.

Educational projects use a large portion of the Ford Foundation's foreign grants. Faculty exchanges are arranged between universities in the United States and those in other countries; fellowships are given to students in the less-developed areas so that they can study in American universities; grants are made to European universities for extended research.

An Institute of Race Relations has been set up in London for making comparative studies in this field. The Foundation assists agricultural development and makes grants to industrial and educational institutions in countries of South and Southeast Asia.

One interesting example of cooperation between the Ford and Rockefeller Foundations is the establishment of a rice institute in the Philippines to increase the quality and amount of the rice produced. Studies are also being made on diseases of the rice plant and its resistance to various pests. The Ford Foundation undertook the initial cost of constructing and equipping the institute, while the Rockefeller Foundation will meet the annual operating expenses and provide the administration.

The two Foundations, although working in different fields and with different methods, have one belief in common. They know that men and women, regardless of race or creed, can work together. They know that fundamentally all persons want to improve their living conditions, that they need more education, and most of all want good health. Each in its own way is trying to help the people of the world to meet these objectives.

Building world friendships

THE PEOPLE-TO-PEOPLE PROGRAM

On September 11, 1956, some fifty leaders, representative of various kinds of occupations, were invited by President Dwight D. Eisenhower to come to Washington. The purpose of this conference was to form a program for a People-to-People partnership.

In his address to the conference, the President stated his belief that all people desire peace. He also told those assembled that there were persons in other parts of the world who were taught that some, and these included Americans, wanted war and that Americans especially were interested in accumulating wealth even though it came from the misery in the world.

He stated that we as Americans are faced with certain problems. First of all, we must find some way to overcome the ignorance about us, presenting our case in such a way that it will strengthen our friendship with those who live in other countries. He emphasized that we have much to learn from these countries, just as they have much to learn from us; and he assured the conference that our government would assist in any way it could, outside of giving financial aid, to help them build a road toward peace. The People-to-People program has been growing and developing ever since.

After President John F. Kennedy came into office he reaffirmed what President Eisenhower had said and on November 8, 1961, he announced that the ex-President had accepted his invitation to serve as honorary chairman of the People-to-People program.

Administering the program is a nonprofit corporation with its headquarters in Kansas City. General Eisenhower is chairman of a board of trustees made up of about a hundred distinguished citizens, and the organization itself is operated by an executive committee of nine members which includes the General because of his office on the larger board.

When the People-to-People program first organized in 1952, about forty committees were formed to include all sorts of activities: Armed Services, Civic, Fraternal Organizations, Hobbies, Letter Writing, Books, Magazines, Medicine and Health, Music, Religious Groups, Travelers, Youth Activities and many others. Working through these committees, many interesting programs developed. An important and wide-spreading one affiliated with the Civic Committee is known as "Twinning."

FRIENDSHIP THROUGH "TWINNING"

In the fall of 1952, in York, Pennsylvania, a new plan of instruction was initiated in the elementary schools. For many years it had been the dream of Dr. Victoria Lyles, the Director of Elementary Education, to have a foreign language taught to the children of the city. Begun as an experiment in one school, with French the language chosen, the program was so successful that the courses soon spread to other schools.

The program in York attracted the attention of the United States Commissioner of Education and York was recommended to Le Monde Bilingue in Paris as being a suitable city to "twin" with a French city.

Le Monde Bilingue, meaning "Two Language World," is an organization which was set up in Paris, France in 1951. Its purpose was to arrange contact between two communities in different countries and to promote exchanges along cultural and industrial lines. It would also encourage correspondence and personal visits between citizens.

The city chosen to "twin" with York was Arles, France, and since that time the friendship between the two cities has deepened. Besides material things, teachers, workers in industries, students and guests are exchanged.

Since that first "twinning" many other cities and towns have adopted the plan. The selection of the "twinning" city is based on mutual interests, size and economic characteristics. Sometimes it is based on historical background and a city in another country is chosen because the original settlers in the American city came from that place. After the selection, contact is made with the American Municipal Association, working with the People-to-People Civic Committee, which has taken over the "twinning" program. Plans for "twinning" are reviewed and assistance with any problems is given.

Sometimes a city chooses a twin because it offers a certain challenge. For example, Darien, Connecticut, chose Mercara, in southwest India. Each year Darien has "India Day" and not only citizens of Darien but many Indians living in the United States participate. The children of Darien can boast, too, that the children of Mercara sent them a baby elephant for the Darien zoo.

Montclair, New Jersey, "twinned" with Graz, Austria, and each year holds a ball to raise money for its "twinning" program.

San José, California, has an affiliation with Okayama, Japan. Many projects are supported by local San José service organizations and the cooperation is so great that San José hotels offer free lodging and auto companies supply free transportation to Okayama visitors.

Cortland, New York, although ten thousand miles away from Peshawar, Pakistan, has established a close relationship with that city. When
the Pakistani government invited the Mayor of Cortland to visit Pakistan, a civic campaign in Cortland raised the money for the trip. And
while he was there, the Mayor of Cortland was elected Honorary
Mayor of Peshawar, the first American to receive that honor.

Since the "twinning" program was initiated, the many cities participating have found new horizons opened to them. Without doubt all
of them have had new and interesting experiences. In two incidents
"twinning" not only helped to form lasting friendships but played the
part of Cupid as well.

Hagerstown, Maryland, is "twinned" with Wesel, Germany. One
year the daughter of the mayor of Hagerstown spent a year as an exchange student in Wesel. While there she met the son of a Wesel judge.
Later he spent a year in Hagerstown and it wasn't long before the two
were married.

Another romance was brought about by "twinning" when York,
Pennsylvania, sent an exchange teacher to Arles, France. She met
the mayor of that city, married him and became Arles' "First Lady."

FRIENDSHIP THROUGH YOUTH EXCHANGE

Although "twinning" has received much national publicity, there
have been other programs established which also have made great
contributions toward understanding between countries. One very important steppingstone on the road toward world peace is an understanding of the countries that make up our world. Our young people
are tomorrow's leaders and because much will depend some day on
their knowledge of the history, culture and problems of their world
neighbors an exchange of youth has been arranged by many countries. In this exchange it is hoped that young people will gain in wisdom and sympathy and be better able to cope with the misinformation
and intolerance they sometimes find at home.

Sometimes students spend a year in another country attending
school. High School students live in private homes; college students
live in the dormitories with other students. But there are other exchange programs too. The 4-H clubs exchange young people who
live and work on the farms of other countries. Boy Scouts and Girl

Scouts arrange for exchanges among their members. Young people attend world conferences of churches and discuss the issues facing youth in this modern world. The Children's International Summer Villages, Inc., in Ohio brings children eleven years of age from a dozen different countries to spend a month in its camp. Recreation leaders are brought from various countries to study recreation in the United States. Young people from other countries are brought to this country to be summer camp counselors. The Catholic Welfare Conference brings children to this country to live for a year with Catholic families and attend school here.

Besides these arranged exchanges of young people, there is another, more informal one. Scattered about over Europe, Canada, South America and the United States are many youth hostels—lodging places for young persons who travel by foot, bicycle, horse or canoe. No automobile travelers are eligible. The hostels, which provide lodging and meals for a very small sum, are supervised by "hostel parents" and the young visitors are welcome to stay for as long as three days if they wish. Here the travelers meet others from different countries, and ideas are exchanged and friendships made. Hosteling opportunities help to encourage the youth of America to travel abroad and those from foreign countries to visit the United States.

All of these projects are important in helping the peoples of the world to learn more about each other.

FRIENDSHIP THROUGH SCIENTIFIC EXCHANGE

During 1957 and 1958 the scientists of the world gave a striking demonstration of how nations can work together when they have a common goal. The period beginning on July 1, 1957, and ending December 31, 1958, was known as the International Geophysical Year, or IGY.

For that one year scientists of the world got together, and in spite of the political rivalries among nations, pooled their knowledge and worked together for mankind.

The IGY was sponsored by the International Council of Scientific Unions and the headquarters for the program were in Uccle, Belgium, a suburb of Brussels. Besides the headquarters in Uccle it was decided to have other centers set up throughout the world where duplicates of the scientific information gathered during this year of research would be housed. That was in case a natural disaster should occur in one of the receiving centers and the information kept there be destroyed.

Although the IGY worked as an independent organization free of governmental control, its success, of course, was dependent on the various governments participating. The countries involved had to permit scientists free entrance and exit from their countries as the need arose. In the United States the cooperation given the IGY was nation-wide. Congress appropriated forty-three million dollars in support of the program. Our military services aided in establishing the Antarctic bases where the scientific studies were to be carried on. Universities, research laboratories, foundations and individual scientists all contributed their services to the cause.

The scientists taking part in the IGY were interested in studying many physical things which affect the whole world, including earthquakes, oceans, weather and solar activity.

During IGY approximately seventy nations took some part in the program, with sixty-six actively participating. The program each country followed differed according to the location and resources.

One of the achievements of that year was the successful launching of artificial satellites. Although Australia, England, Canada, France, Japan, the United States and the Soviet Union contributed to the study, the U.S.S.R. and the United States were the only two that actually launched satellites, because they had made previous experiments. However, many other nations cooperated by providing tracking stations.

All nations participated in studying weather conditions and many new discoveries were made, ranging from ocean currents to radiation zones in space.

Information was gathered about Antarctica also, to determine what effect that ice-bound continent had on the weather of the whole world, and it was decided to continue the study after the IGY. After the first year Norway decided to drop out, which left eleven nations to carry on: Argentina, Australia, Belgium, Chile, France, Japan, New Zealand, the Soviet Union, the Union of South Africa, the United Kingdom and the United States.

On December 1, 1959, all twelve countries, including Norway, signed the Antarctica Treaty, guaranteeing that Antarctica will always be used for peaceful purposes. The Treaty is to last indefinitely, but after thirty years any nation may ask to have it revised.

Just as important as the actual scientific discoveries made concerning space, land and under-ocean conditions is the fact that world scientists have found satisfaction in working together.

FRIENDSHIP THROUGH CULTURAL EXCHANGE

Cultural exchanges have played their part, too, in helping to create good will and understanding among peoples of different nationalities. One type of exchange between nations that has been successful for many years is the holding of a fair or exhibition. The first forerunner of our present-day World's Fair was held in London in 1753. A fair in Paris in 1889 built as its central structure the Eiffel Tower, which was left standing and has become that city's most famous landmark. The first fair of national importance in the United States was held in New York City in 1853, in Bryant Park, which is just behind the New York Public Library at Fifth Avenue and Forty-second Street.

For a long time fairs celebrated anniversaries and national events, but in recent years the emphasis has been on the world of the future, and many more countries participate. Architects design elaborate pavilions where they can display and publicize the best their country offers in products, scientific progress and culture. Although the displays are expensive, most countries feel it is worth while to be represented among the nations of the world. What is very important, the fairs are visited by people from all over the world and the holiday mood creates a feeling of mutual respect and understanding.

Fairs represent cultural exchange on a huge scale. More individual in nature are the arrangements made between two countries for an exchange of artistic talent. Since 1955, for example, the United States and the Soviet Union have had an agreement of this kind.

On our part we have sent over such distinguished performers as the *Porgy and Bess* company which made a great hit with Moscow audiences. The Boston Symphony, the Philadelphia Orchestra and the New York Philharmonic have also been welcomed in the U.S.S.R. *Holiday on Ice,* starring the former Olympic champion Dick Button, was greeted with enthusiasm. Such individual stars as violinist Isaac Stern and singers Jan Peerce, Marian Anderson and Roberta Peters contributed to the establishing of a person-to-person friendship.

One of the artists most enthusiastically acclaimed by the Russians was the young American pianist, Harvey Lavan Cliburn, better known as Van Cliburn. Van Cliburn was born in Shreveport, Louisiana, but later moved to Kilgore, Texas. Van's mother was a former concert pianist and she began teaching piano to her young son when he was only three years old. After he was older he studied at the Juilliard School of Music in New York City.

In 1958, Van Cliburn entered the International Tchaikovsky Competition in Moscow along with competitors from nineteen countries. Somehow this young attractive American completely captured the hearts of the Russians and he was very popular with them. When he won the contest he was rousingly cheered by the Moscow audience. On his return to the United States he was received with enthusiasm by his own countrymen as well. New York City gave him one of its famous ticker-tape parades, the first one ever accorded a musician.

Visits from Russian performers to this country have been equally welcomed on this side of the Atlantic. The American debuts of pianist Emil Gilels and violinist David Oistrakh had fine audience response. One company that especially captivated Americans was the Moiseyev Dancers, who specialize in folk dances. Their performances were colorful, brilliant and theatrical, and they were practically mobbed in every city they played on tour. The fact that they were also seen on television made them well known throughout the country.

Probably the Russian company which climaxed this exchange was the Bolshoi Ballet. The Bolshoi Ballet had never performed outside the U.S.S.R. except in London, Paris and Brussels. The word "Bolshoi" in Russian means "big." And "big" certainly described this company of one hundred dancers.

The Bolshoi made its debut in this country at the Metropolitan Opera House. From the time the announcement was made of its coming the box office was swamped with many more requests for tickets than it could possibly fill. Because of the elaborate stage settings required for its performances, it did not play in as many cities as the Moiseyev Dancers and not as many people saw it, but the publicity it received throughout the country was great.

On March 8, 1962, a new two-year agreement was signed by the two powerful rivals to expand their cultural exchanges. Among other American artists named to visit the Soviet Union were the Robert Shaw Chorale and the Benny Goodman Orchestra. It was the first time a jazz orchestra had been officially accepted by the Russians. The Russians agreed to a return visit of the Bolshoi Ballet. The Leningrad Philharmonic Symphony Orchestra and the Ukrainian Dance Ensemble were also to tour several cities of the United States.

FRIENDSHIP THROUGH GOVERNMENT AID

The Marshall Plan

When World War II ended in 1945, many of the cities of Europe had been left in utter ruin. Bombs had made great craters and buildings everywhere had been leveled. Industrial plants were destroyed; transportation lines were disrupted; many persons were homeless. Fields that had formerly grown crops were covered with the debris left over from battles. Food supplies were low and in some countries people existed on the barest of rations. Goods that ordinarily are manufactured for the daily use of people were not available because the factories had been put to wartime use. It was a time of discouragement.

Hunger and insecurity are hard on people. They become restive and are ready for any sort of change that they hope will better their condition. It was necessary for the governments of these countries to see to it that rebuilding and restoring normal conditions be started. But to do this required money—much of it—and there was a scarcity of that too.

On June 5, 1947, Secretary of State George C. Marshall, in a speech at Harvard University, made an important statement which was to have a strong impact on the rest of the world.

Secretary Marshall proposed that the United States extend financial aid to any European country "willing to assist in the task of recovery." Soon after this proposal the United States Congress appropriated some twelve billion dollars to be spent over the next three and a half years on devastated European countries which met the requirement of being willing to assist themselves at the same time.

The Marshall Plan was the forerunner of future aid plans to countries all over the world. It assisted European countries that needed help badly to get back on their feet, with restored confidence in themselves, and it turned back the wave of Communism which was threatening to sweep over Europe.

The Point Four Program

On January 20, 1949, about a year and a half after the beginning of the Marshall Plan, President Harry Truman was making his inaugural address on the steps of the Capitol in Washington.

As point four in his speech he announced that the United States was planning to establish a program of technical assistance to the undeveloped parts of the world.

He said the purpose of this program was to "help the free peoples of the world, through their own efforts, to produce more food, more clothing, more materials for housing, and more mechanical power to lighten their burdens." He said that by doing all this the United States would be helping to promote peace and make it possible for all men to have "freedom and dignity and fullness of life."

For many years a number of organizations had been working along this line. Missionary groups had been helping the people in the countries where they were stationed, and American industries with plants in far-off places were doing the same thing, but this was the first time that such aid was recognized as a part of United States foreign policy.

Point Four worked like this:

1. The request for assistance had to come from the government involved, explaining just what kind of aid it wanted. Then the United States had to check with various agencies of the United Nations and with other organizations such as the Rockefeller and Ford Foundations to be sure the same job was not being done by them.

2. United States Government agencies and universities all over the country were combed to see if there were any workers qualified for the jobs to be done.

3. These workers were sent out to the country asking for assistance, not only to work but to train someone there to take over the job later on.

It was hoped that this program of close cooperation between friendly countries would strengthen democracy throughout the world by helping the people toward a better life and giving them hope for the future. It would benefit a country in a material way, too, for it would assist in developing the raw materials the nation needed for world trade.

The Peace Corps

During Senator John F. Kennedy's campaign for the Presidency in 1960, he spoke of reports he had heard from Congressmen who had traveled in countries receiving our technical assistance. The suggestion had been made that what was needed more than general aid such as road building was personal advice of the kind one farmer might give to another. Senator Kennedy said in his speech, "I therefore propose that our inadequate efforts in this area be supplemented by a Peace Corps of talented young men [he later added "and women"] who are able and willing to serve their country . . . well qualified by rigorous standards, well trained in the languages, skills and customs they will need to know. This would be a volunteer corps from every race and walk of life."

The next January at his inauguration he offered this challenge: "Ask not what your country will do for you—ask what you can do for your country."

On March 1, 1961, the Peace Corps was established by executive order. By March 1, 1962, after its first year of operation, 880 young people had answered the challenge offered by the President in his inaugural address and had been accepted as Peace Corps workers.

The idea underlying the Peace Corps is that new nations need many services but there is a scarcity of trained native workers to accomplish them. The Peace Corps does not try to take over the field from any other organization that is already trying to help, and it goes in only where it has been requested. The type of work varies a great deal—teaching, agriculture, public health, sanitation, home economics —and skilled craftsmen such as auto mechanics, carpenters, masons and plumbers are just a few of the types needed.

Although many of the young people applying for the Corps are college graduates, a college education is not a requirement. Many skilled workers in crafts or trades are badly needed. Leadership is one of the main qualities that count.

The training period usually lasts anywhere from two to six months before the Corps members are sent out. During this period they study the host nation's language, history, customs and economic conditions, and if volunteers are skilled in some particular craft, they are given a refresher course in that, too.

The Corps members are aware that they are representatives of their country and they know they must be able to discuss intelligently any questions their hosts ask about our history, our government, our politics and our way of life.

At the end of the first year, although it had had some criticism, the Peace Corps had become accepted both at home and abroad. In its first twelve months of existence, one thousand corpsmen were serving in thirteen countries, and every nation using Peace Corps aid had requested more.

Because it had been so well received abroad, Congress passed new legislation to continue its existence in April, 1962. In the Senate the bill was passed without a dissenting vote. The House passed the appropriation for the Corps by a vote of 361 to 70.

The young Americans serving abroad in the Peace Corps have had high goals set before them. They have had to demonstrate their technical and professional skills under new conditions. What is more important, they have had to conduct themselves by their behavior and by their words in such a way that they bring their hosts the true spirit of America.

FRIENDSHIP THROUGH ORGANIZATIONS

Not everyone can travel as a member of the Youth Exchange program and not everyone is lucky enough to have a foreign visitor in his home or to be a member of the Peace Corps, but there is still a lot to be learned by working through home organizations.

Young people's groups can work out their own programs to help their members gain more knowledge of their world neighbors. Programs can be arranged featuring games, songs, stories and even food typical of other countries. Special holidays which are important to other countries can be celebrated. Talks by community residents from other countries can stimulate interest in foreign lands.

Young people can participate in other ways, too, in the People-to-People program. The Magazine and Book Committees welcome book drives to help supply their need for overseas distribution. Of course the books and magazines sent are carefully selected, not only for their particular subject material but for their interest to both adults and children. The busy Hobbies Committee puts people in touch with others around the world who share the same hobby.

The Letter Writing Committee helps stay-at-homes develop world-wide friendships. The United States Information Service has said that this is one way an individual can add to our country's program of mutual understanding. Usually the contacts with persons of another country are made through an organization. Schools, Girl Scouts, Boy Scouts, 4-H Clubs, Camp Fire Girls, Future Homemakers of America and many others have regular letter-writing projects. The purpose is to learn what life is like in another country. Young Americans should never forget that through their letters they are giving their foreign friends a picture of the United States.

FRIENDSHIP THROUGH INDIVIDUALS

A single person can be the means of creating a good or a bad feeling toward America. When American tourists go abroad their attitude toward their host countries is most important. Audible unfavorable comparisons of another country most decidedly will not make friends for us. And it is just as important to make foreign visitors to our country, no matter what their national background may be, feel as welcome and as comfortable as possible.

Today there are many Americans whose businesses require that they live abroad. They are our unofficial overseas ambassadors. Their ability to respect the customs of the country in which they are living and to treat its citizens with consideration will go a long way toward creating a favorable impression of the United States there. One arrogant person can do our country much harm.

The United States has armed forces stationed in many parts of the world, and we must not forget that some people living in those countries resent this fact. Americans in uniform have it in their power to create a favorable or unfavorable impression of the United States. In Vendrell, Spain, some members of our armed forces stationed at the nearby Sargossa air base will always be remembered with gratitude.

In that little Spanish village there was a statue of the Angel Gabriel perched on the top of the village church. The statue, which weighed more than three hundred pounds, had been standing on the bell tower for several centuries, and one day someone noticed that it had begun to teeter. There was great consternation until the mayor had an inspiration. He notified officers at the air base of the village's predicament and immediately the Air Force went into action, sending a helicopter to the rescue. The statue was removed from its place on the bell tower and brought down for repairs. When the helicopter lifted it back once again to its resting place, the Sixth Fleet band cheered on the operation with appropriate triumphal music! The photographs taken of "Operation helicopter" were distributed all over Spain, and the courtesy of our Air Force in that one small incident made lots of friends for our country.

What one single individual can do toward creating good will is shown most dramatically in the story of Harry Morgan.

Harry, nineteen years old, was working in a sugar mill near Salinas, California. One day he happened to read in a newspaper an account of the terrific floods in Holland in which thousands of people had lost their homes.

Somehow the story had a profound effect on the young man. Filled with compassion for all those desolate people, he was determined to help them in some way.

Harry didn't have much money, but he made it do as he hitchhiked across the country to New York. He stopped off in Chicago on the way and was fortunate enough to get on the radio program "Welcome Traveler," which gave free breakfasts to guests who had been interviewed. When Harry told his story and what he planned to do, the interviewer was so impressed that Harry got not only his breakfast but free air passage from New York to Amsterdam.

In Amsterdam Harry got in touch with the local office of the Friends Service Committee, which arranged for him to go to Rotterdam. Volunteer workers there were in the process of cleaning up the debris from the flood.

Harry was a friendly young man and the Hollanders welcomed him gladly. They were amazed, too, because many of them had thought of teen-age Americans as belonging to gangs and out to make trouble. Harry's fame spread as his story was printed in the papers and as he traveled from village to village wherever his help was needed.

Soon after Harry returned to the United States, he enlisted in the Air Force and was stationed near Dayton, Ohio. During the next three years he devoted his spare time to making speeches in churches and civic clubs about his visit to Holland and the friendliness he had found there. On one of his leaves he went back to Holland to visit his friends.

When he returned to the United States he got the idea of raising enough money to bring two Hollanders to this country for a visit. He asked some Dayton businessmen for contributions and when he had enough he made his choice of guests. He wanted particularly to choose two who had been most skeptical when he had told them about life in America. One person he invited was a young woman schoolteacher and the other was a garbage collector.

When his visitors arrived he arranged for them to be taken on a round of visits to factories, farms, town meetings, church suppers, family parties, homes of those in humble circumstances and homes of those who were well-to-do. Everywhere they found friendliness and when they returned to Holland they couldn't say enough in praise of Americans.

As the story of the Hollanders' visit gained publicity in the United States, Harry began to receive letters from people asking that they be included the next time he was seeking contributions for such a project. This made him realize that probably many more would be interested in doing the same thing.

So he formed "Ambassadors for Friendship" and soon money began to pour in. When he thought he had enough, he again went to Europe, and this time he appealed to the United States Information Agency for help. Together they screened candidates and finally came up with four: a twenty-year-old girl bank clerk from Graz, Austria; a furniture salesman from Copenhagen, Denmark; an apprentice engineer from Augsburg, Germany; and an air-transportation trainee from Annecy, France.

When these young people came to the United States they were

given the opportunity to see everything they wanted to. They saw the worst along with the best. Because our racial problems have been given wide publicity abroad, the guests were given the opportunity to talk to Negroes and learn firsthand what racial relations are like in this country. And when these four persons went back to their own countries they were able to give a fair account of what conditions were in the United States.

Later, Harry Morgan enrolled as a student at Rutgers University in New Brunswick, New Jersey, where he met a student from India whose opinion of America was anything but complimentary. Harry found that his whole judgment was based on a small knowledge of what really constituted America. He had never been farther away from New Brunswick than New York City.

Harry was appalled to discover that while we were conducting an exchange student program, we were not being careful to see that the foreign students experienced what was good in this country as well as what was bad. There was still about $1000 left in the Ambassadors for Friendship fund, so he decided to invite four students to tour America with him. The American Motor Company became so interested in his project that it offered to supply him with a car. Then came the problem of whom he should select to make this trip. His first choice was easy: the young Indian who had such a poor opinion of America. He next chose a young Italian student whose home town in Italy was made up largely of Communists. Then came an art student from the Philippines whose sketches of New York life intended for a Manila newspaper were more caricatures than portraits. His fourth choice was a civil engineering student from Argentina who was a student at Columbia University and who had never been outside of New York.

The tour took them through thirty-eight states. They went to Washington, D.C., and to historic Williamsburg. They were received by America's great poet Carl Sandburg. They went to Little Rock, Arkansas, known throughout the world for the racial violence which took place when its schools were first integrated. They attended church clambakes, P.T.A. meetings and baseball games. They went to political rallies where people spoke their minds freely. They talked to labor management leaders. They visited museums, art galleries and libraries. They stayed at hotels or at farmhouses, wherever they happened to be at night. They saw America as it really is. And when the tour was over each one admitted that his ideas of America had changed, and that he was eager to go home and tell what he had seen.

"Twinning," Youth Exchange, Cultural and Scientific Exchange, government aid, organization plans and individual efforts—all these ways of spreading friendship are important. However small the gesture may seem when we stretch out a welcoming hand to someone from another country, we must remember we are making that gesture of brotherhood in the name of our country.

Bibliography

ADDAMS, JANE. *Forty Years at Hull House.* New York: The Macmillan Company, 1935.

American Peoples Encyclopedia. Chicago: The Spencer Press, Inc., 1956
———. Yearbook. Chicago: The Spencer Press, Inc., 1960, 1961.

ANDERSON, ERICA AND EXMAN, EUGENE. *The World of Albert Schweitzer.* New York: Harper & Brothers, 1955.

ANDERSON, MARIAN. *My Lord, What a Morning.* New York: Viking Press, 1956.

ANDREWS, C. F., ed. *Mahatma Gandhi: His Own Story.* New York: The Macmillan Company, 1930.

ANSLEY, DELIGHT. *The Good Ways.* New York: Thomas Y. Crowell Company, 1950.

BARTLETT, JOHN. *Familiar Quotations.* New York: Little, Brown and Company, 1955.

BARTLETT, ROBERT MERRILL. *They Dare to Believe.* New York: Association Press, 1952.

BERRILL, JACQUELINE. *Albert Schweitzer: Man of Mercy.* New York: Dodd, Mead & Company, Inc., 1956.

BOURKE-WHITE, MARGARET. *Halfway to Freedom.* New York: Simon and Schuster, 1949.

CARUS, PAUL. *The Gospel of Buddha According to Old Records.* The Open Court Publishing Company, Chicago.

CAUDWELL, IRENE. *Damien of Molokai—1840–1889.* New York: The Macmillan Company, 1932.

COCHRANE, JOANNA. *Let's Go to the United Nations Headquarters.* New York: G. P. Putnam's Sons, 1958.

COUSINS, NORMAN. *Dr. Schweitzer of Lambaréné.* New York: Harper & Brothers, 1960.

COYLE, DAVID CUSHMAN. *The United Nations and How It Works.* New York: Columbia Press, 1961.

Current Biography. New York: H. W. Wilson Company, 1943.

DANIEL, ANITA. *The Story of Albert Schweitzer.* New York: Random House, Inc., 1957.

DOOLEY, THOMAS A. *Deliver Us from Evil.* New York: Farrar, Straus & Cudahy, Inc., 1956.

DOOLEY, THOMAS A. *The Edge of Tomorrow*. New York: Farrar, Straus & Cudahy, Inc., 1958.

————. *The Night They Burned the Mountain*. New York: Farrar, Straus & Cudahy, Inc., 1960.

DUFFUS, R. L. *Lillian Wald*. New York: The Macmillan Company, 1938.

EDWARDS, CLAYTON. *A Treasury of Heroes and Heroines*. New York: Frederick A. Stokes Company, 1920.

EICHELBERGER, CLARK M. *U. N. The First Fifteen Years*. New York: Harper & Brothers, 1960.

Encyclopaedia Britannica. Encyclopaedia Britannica, Inc. Chicago: William Benton, 1961.

EPSTEIN, EDNA. *The First Book of the United Nations*. New York: Franklin Watts, Inc., 1959.

ERDMAN, WALTER C. *Sources of Power in Famous Lives*. Nashville: Cokesbury Press, 1936.

ERVINE, ST. JOHN. *God's Soldier: General William Booth*. New York: The Macmillan Company, 1935. 2 volumes.

FISCHER, LOUIS. *The Life of Mahatma Gandhi*. New York: Harper & Brothers, 1950.

FITCH, FLORENCE MARY. *Allah, The God of Islam*. New York: Lothrop, Lee & Shepard Co., Inc., 1950.

————. *One God*. New York: Lothrop, Lee & Shepard Co., Inc., 1944.

————. *Their Search for God*. New York: Lothrop, Lee & Shepard Co., Inc., 1947.

FOSDICK, RAYMOND B. *Story of the Rockefeller Foundation*. New York: Harper & Brothers, 1952.

FRANCK, FREDERICK. *Days with Albert Schweitzer*. New York: Henry Holt & Co., 1959.

GALLANCZ, VICTOR. *Man and God*. Boston: Houghton Mifflin Company, 1951.

HAGEDORN, HERMANN. *The Book of Courage*. Philadelphia: The John C. Winston Company, 1930.

HALL, ANNA GERTRUDE. *Nansen*. New York: The Viking Press, 1940.

HINSHAW, DAVID. *Herbert Hoover: American Quaker*. New York: Farrar, Straus & Company, 1950.

HUGHES, LANGSTON. *Famous American Negroes*. New York: Dodd, Mead & Company, Inc., 1954.

HUNTER, ALLAN A. *Three Trumpets Sound. Kagawa—Gandhi—Schweitzer*. New York: Association Press, 1939.

HUNTING, HAROLD B. *Marian Anderson, Singer*. (in) Lotz, Philip Henry. *Rising Above Color*. New York: Fleming H. Revell, 1943.

HUROK, SOL. *Impresario*. New York: Random House, 1946.

JONES, JESSIE ORTON. *This Is the Way*. New York: The Viking Press, 1951.

JOY, CHARLES R., ed. *Albert Schweitzer: An Anthology*. New York: Harper & Brothers, 1947.

KEENY, SPURGEON MILTON. *Half the World's Children.* New York: Association Press, 1957.

KENWORTHY, LEONARD S. *Twelve Citizens of the World.* Garden City: Doubleday and Co., Inc., 1953.

KNAPP, SALLY. *Eleanor Roosevelt.* New York: Thomas Y. Crowell Co., 1949.

KUGELMASS, J. ALVIN. *Ralph J. Bunche: Fighter for Peace.* New York: Julian Messner, Inc., 1952.

LARSEN, EGON. *Men Who Shaped the Future.* New York: Roy Publishers, 1957.

LASH, JOSEPH P. *Dag Hammarskjold.* Garden City: Doubleday and Co., Inc., 1961.

Life Magazine, ed. *The World's Great Religions.* New York: Time, Inc., 1957.

LUDWIG, EMIL. *Nine Etched from Life.* New York: Robert McBride & Company, 1934.

MCNEER, MAY AND WARD, LYND. *Armed With Courage.* Nashville: Abingdon-Cokesbury Press, 1957.

MARSHACK, ALEXANDER. *The World in Space.* New York: Thomas Nelson and Sons, 1958.

PICKETT, CLARENCE E. *For More Than Bread.* New York: Little, Brown & Company, 1953.

PITT, JAMES E. *Adventures in Brotherhood.* New York: Farrar, Straus & Co., Inc., 1955.

RICHARDSON, BEN. *Great American Negroes.* New York: Thomas Y. Crowell Co., 1945.

RIIS, JACOB A. *The Battle with the Slum.* New York: The Macmillan Company, 1902.

———. *How the Other Half Lives.* New York: Charles Scribner's Sons, 1918.

———. *The Making of an American.* New York: The Macmillan Company, 1901.

ROOSEVELT, ELEANOR. *"Human Rights."* (in) Lie, Trygve and others. *Peace on Earth.* New York: Hermitage House, 1949.

———. *If You Ask Me.* New York: D. Appleton–Century Company, Inc., 1946.

———. *On My Own.* New York: Harper & Brothers, 1958.

———. *This I Remember.* New York: Harper & Brothers, 1949.

———. *This Is My Story.* New York: Garden City Pub. Co., 1937.

———. *You Learn By Living.* New York: Harper & Brothers, 1960.

——— and FERRIS, HELEN. *Partners: The United Nations and Youth.* Garden City: Doubleday and Co., Inc., 1950.

SCHULL, REBECCA. *Government At Work.* New York: Sterling Pub. Co., 1962.

SCHWEITZER, ALBERT. *Out of My Life and Thought.* An Autobiography. New York: Henry Holt & Co., 1933, 1949.

———. *The Problem of Peace in the World Today.* Chicago: Albert Schweitzer Education Foundation, 1959.

SEAGRAVE, GORDON S. *Burma Surgeon.* New York: W. W. Norton & Co., Inc., 1943.

———. *Burma Surgeon Returns.* New York: W. W. Norton & Co., Inc., 1946.

———. *My Hospital in the Hills.* New York: W. W. Norton & Co., Inc., 1955.

SHEEHAN, ARTHUR and SHEEHAN, ELIZABETH ODELL. *Father Damien and the Bells.* New York: Farrar, Straus & Co., Inc., 1957.

SHEEHAN, VINCENT. *Mahatma Gandhi: A Great Life in Brief.* New York: Alfred A. Knopf, 1955.

SHRIDHARANI, KRISHNALAL. *The Mahatma and the World.* New York: Duell, Sloan and Pearce, 1946.

SORENSEN, JON. *The Saga of Fridtjof Nansen,* translated from the Norwegian by J. B. C. Watkins. New York: The American Scandinavian Foundation and W. W. Norton & Company, Inc., 1932.

STEINBERG, ALFRED. *Mrs. R: the Life of Eleanor Roosevelt.* New York: G. P. Putnam's Sons, Inc., 1958.

STERLING, DOROTHY. *United Nations, N. Y.* Garden City: Doubleday and Co., Inc., 1953.

STEVENS, WILLIAM OLIVER. *Famous Humanitarians.* New York: Dodd Mead & Co., Inc., 1953.

SULLIVAN, WALTER. *Assault on the Unknown.* New York: McGraw-Hill Book Co., Inc., 1961.

SZYMCZAK, CHESTER J. *When Time Stood Still.* Philadelphia: Dorrance & Company, Inc., 1956.

THOMAS, EDWARD J. *The Life of Buddha.* New York: Alfred A. Knopf, 1927.

THOMAS, HENRY AND THOMAS, DANA LEE. *50 Great Americans.* Garden City: Doubleday and Co., Inc., 1948.

THORNTON, FRANCIS B. *Sea of Glory: the Magnificent Story of the Four Chaplains.* New York: Prentice-Hall, Inc., 1953.

TIMS, MARGARET. *Jane Addams of Hull House 1860–1935.* New York: The Macmillan Company, 1961.

VEHANAN, KOSTI. *Marian Anderson; a Portrait.* New York: McGraw-Hill (Whittlesey House), 1941.

WADE, MARY H. *Pilgrims of Today.* Boston: Little, Brown & Co., 1934.

WALD, LILLIAN D. *The House on Henry Street.* New York: Henry Holt & Co., 1915.

———. *Windows on Henry Street.* Boston: Little, Brown & Co., 1936.

WARE, LOUISE. *Jacob A. Riis.* New York: D. Appleton–Century Co., 1938

WILLIAMS, BERYL. *Lillian Wald; Angel of Henry Street.* New York: Julian Messner, Inc., 1948.

WILSON, P. WHITWELL. *General Evangeline Booth.* New York: Fleming H. Revell Company, 1935.

WISE, WINIFRED E. *Jane Addams of Hull House.* New York: Harcourt, Brace & Co., Inc., 1935.

World Almanac. New York: New York World-Telegram, 1961, 1962.

World Book Encyclopedia. Chicago: Field Enterprises Educational Corp., 1962.

YATES, ELIZABETH. *Rainbow Round the World: A Story of UNICEF.* Indianapolis: The Bobbs-Merrill Company, 1954.

YOST, EDNA. *American Women of Nursing.* Philadelphia: J. B. Lippincott Co., 1947.

Also numerous annual reports of organizations, pamphlets, transcripts of speeches, magazine and newspaper articles.

Index

219

ABOUT THE AUTHORS

ELIZABETH HOUGH SECHRIST became interested in writing for children while she was a children's librarian in Bethlehem, Pennsylvania. Each year she was asked by boys and girls, teachers and librarians, for information on Christmas in other lands. Because of the lack of material, she began to collect and write on the subject herself, and the resulting book, *Christmas Everywhere,* has been popular in schools and libraries for many years.

After nine years' experience in Bethlehem and Pittsburgh libraries, Mrs. Sechrist gave up her work to devote her time to writing, editing and lecturing on children's books—and incidentally to keeping house. In York, Pennsylvania, where she and her husband live, a collection of cookbooks is conspicuous on the shelves along with those on birds, animals and furniture.

JANETTE WOOLSEY is a librarian at the Martin Memorial Library in York, Pennsylvania. One summer her library program was a marionette theater, and it was during this time that she became interested in play production and writing. She and the children wrote the plays and presented them to a capacity audience each week. Miss Woolsey is a graduate of Middlebury College, Pratt Institute and Columbia University. She started her library career as children's librarian at Ohio University. She lives in York, and devotes much of her free time to lecturing on children's books and storytelling.